DECIPHERING
ANGEL NUMBERS

DECIPHERING
ANGEL NUMBERS

TRANSLATE YOUR
GUARDIANS' MESSAGES

✦ ✦ ✦ ✦

APRIL WALL

weldon**owen**

CONTENTS

INTRODUCTION

EVER NOTICE A NUMBER that seems to pop out at you over and over again? Think of a typical day. You check the time. It's 11:11. You need to head into town to get your to-do list handled. You start with a little lunch. It totals $11.11. Hmm, didn't you see that number earlier? You sprint around town running errands. As you do, your mind is awhirl with the new business you recently started. You're unsure whether it was the best idea to chase your dreams instead of keeping your job in finance. When you return home, you notice that two of your receipts have that number again: 11.11. What's the deal? Is the Universe trying to tell you something? The short answer is, yes!

If you've never heard of angel numbers, but resonate with the scenario just described, whether you knew it or not, you have come into contact with those magical numbers. "Angel numbers" is the popular term coined for communication between the spiritual realm and us. In our society, it's common to think of otherworldly guardians and helpers as angels. Thus, the term "angel numbers" was born. But angel numbers are universal—they don't belong to any one religion or spiritual path. This type of communication is open to all, regardless of belief system.

We're all equipped with a spirit team upon entry into this world. That team is made up of angels or guardians, guides, ancestors, and loved ones in spirit. These soul people have our best interests at heart. They work to look after, guide, and protect us at pivotal moments in our lives. And we have the ability to communicate with these beings without utilizing any special type of psychic or magical skill. Because our spirit team loves us unconditionally and roots for our success, of course, they want to give us messages of hope and encouragement when we need them.

So, you might be thinking, *Why communicate through numbers?* Well, let's think this through. How would you respond if an otherworldly, ethereal being suddenly appeared in front of you? Not only might you pass out from shock, but would you really trust that it even happened? As soon as you came to, you'd immediately start listing reasons to excuse away the experience. Must have been dreaming. Maybe a little too much wine with dinner. But, instead, there's an intelligence to Spirit. They know how to send us information in the best way for us to receive it.

In 1952, British scientist Lancelot Hogben pointed out that a number is the most universal concept for establishing communication between intelligent beings. His theory formed the basis for the first steps in extraterrestrial communication. Numbers are a universal language. If we can use them to communicate with ET, certainly we can use them to communicate with our spirit team.

Angel numbers aren't a random assortment of numbers. They are unique numbers that have the ability to catch our attention and communicate information. No easy feat in today's world of constant digital entertainment, but that's what makes them so special. They contain either repetition, patterns, or sequences that make them stand out. With an infinite amount of numbers to choose from, our angels have narrowed it down to those they know we'll pay attention to, even amid the chaos of daily life.

For years, I've offered insight into the recurring numbers my clients have seen during their psychic readings with me. It is one of the many tools I employ as a psychic medium to help my sitters receive the information they seek. Fortune-telling, or *dukkering* as it is known in the Romany language, is one of the main ways my people were able to make a living while moving from place to place. As both Romany and a psychic medium, all forms of divinatory arts are important to me. Not only did the Romany help spread these practices, but we firmly put our stamp on them. In fact, every Hollywood movie you have ever seen featuring divination probably involves a Gypsy stereotype. With this book, it is my goal not only to teach you about angel numbers, but also to use my voice to make sure the Romany people and our role within divination arts are represented and respected. **Note:** The term "Gypsy" is considered a slur and should not be used by non-Romany people.

Ahead is all the information you'll need to decipher angel numbers. I have structured this book to take you through the process step by step, each chapter building upon the previous. We will look first at the history of numbers in chapter 1. Then, we'll find out who sends those mysterious and timely numerical messages in chapter 2. By chapter 3, you'll learn about all the different ways in which to receive angel numbers. Chapter 4 gives you a glossary of more than 120 angel numbers to begin deciphering for your life, broken down into easy-to-use categories. We finish by learning about even more options for incorporating angel numbers into your daily life—from manifesting to choosing important dates in chapter 5.

CHAPTER 1

A BRIEF HISTORY
OF NUMEROLOGY

T O UNDERSTAND ANGEL numbers, it's helpful to understand the very nature of numbers, which can be done through numerology, the study of the mystical significance of numbers. Numbers are the building blocks of our world. Truly, everything around us depends on the use of numbers. Cooking food requires numbers. They are needed to construct every building. Numbers run our economies. We measure our lives in numbers as clocks keep up with the passage of time. Numbers aren't just a construct left behind when we finished high school math. They are inherently built into the very fabric of the universe. So, what's the connection between numbers and angel communication? Let's take a look back to the guy who got all this number madness going, Pythagoras.

In the sixth century BCE, Pythagoras was a lover of numbers. More specifically, he was a Greek philosopher, mathematician, and mystic. Most numerologists credit him with being the founder of numerology, or at the very least, the person who brought it to light in ancient Greece, though earlier civilizations, such as the Sumerians and Maya people, invented numerical systems and used numbers as a way of timing sacred events.

Pythagoras had a group of followers, known as Pythagoreans, who studied mathematics, music, philosophy, and more. They lived together in a secret society where they believed all things were made of numbers. This may come as a surprise to you if your only introduction to Pythagoras was in geometry class, learning the Pythagorean theorem: $a^2 + b^2 = c^2$. In fact, Pythagoras may not have invented this famous formula, but that's for another day. What's important is that Pythagoras established a foundation for understanding that numbers had their own individual vibrations and frequencies. It was his belief that the planets and stars moved according to mathematical equations that corresponded to musical notes and produced an inaudible symphony. In this way, you can imagine that everything works in perfect harmony, all through the power of numbers.

Pythagoras's ideas about numbers are the foundation of this current concept of numerology and angel numbers. He believed that odd numbers were masculine, whereas even numbers were feminine, which corresponds to our modern ideas of the Divine Feminine represented in the number 2 and the Divine Masculine represented by the number 3. He considered 10 to be a perfect number, as the sequence $1 + 2 + 3 + 4$ led to its creation. He saw it represented in a human's ten fingers and toes. Due to its perfection in his eyes, he and his followers never gathered in groups larger than ten. Truly, Pythagoras serves as the great-grandfather to the modern numerology movement.

As we make our way through history, it would take quite a while before Pythagoras's ideas about numbers would come to the forefront again—not until the nineteenth century, through the help of author L. Dow Balliett. She wrote several books on the subject of numbers, including *The Philosophy of Numbers: Their Tone and Colors*, which many still refer to today. It was her belief, using Pythagoras's teachings as a guide, that numbers held specific colors, sounds, and vibrations. Although her teachings aren't really practiced today, she had an effect on the study of numbers. In both Pythagoras's and Mrs. Balliett's teachings, the numbers 1–9 were each given a specific meaning, which guide our angel number definitions today.

In more recent times, Glynis McCants, known as "the Numbers Lady," has added more teaching and information to the field of numerology through her numerous books and offerings.

Through numbers, one can determine potential compatibility with a romantic partner, which numbers can be deemed lucky, even the trajectory of one's life. Our angelic partners in the spiritual realm take that built-in knowledge and wisdom and use numbers as a way to get our attention and communicate more effectively with us in this modern, technology-obsessed world. Let's learn more about those entities who send these special messages now!

CHAPTER 2

WHO SENDS ANGEL NUMBERS?

THIS MAY SEEM self-explanatory, but who, exactly, sends these angel numbers to us? Angels are spiritual beings who have never walked earth or lived a human life. They are discarnate souls who are made up of the spiritual force of the Universe, which is love. As mentioned earlier, we are all assigned a spirit team upon incarnation to earth. A part of that team is angels. They are allowed to guide, protect, and instruct us, but never in a way that removes free will or alters the course we've chosen in life. They are by our sides from the moment we enter this life until we exit it, through many lifetimes over.

Although the term "angel numbers" is used to describe the communication sent by guardian spirits, these signs can also be sent by others on your spirit team, such as your ancestors, guides, and even loved ones in spirit. Pay attention to other signs and symbols you receive when you see angel numbers as they can give you a specific idea of who is behind the message. Ultimately, all of this information comes from a force I refer to as "Spirit." You may call it "Source," a "Higher Power," or "God." All names can be used interchangeably, and are throughout this book.

Many times, I see the number 304, and I know it's a message from my best friend, Kristy, who left this world too soon, at the young age of nineteen. When we were in high school, beepers, or pagers, were all the rage, but pagers allowed you only to leave your number so someone could call you back. Nowhere near as convenient as texting is now, we used numbers as shortcuts for words. "Hello" was 07734, which you could make out when turned upside down. "Call me now" came in as 911. "I love you" was 143. And if you shared Kristy's and my sense of humor, 304 meant "hoe," which we would call each other affectionately. What can I say? We were '90s babies. Now, every time I see that number, I know my dear friend is sending a special hello, which usually comes when I need a laugh.

As stated earlier, we have a spirit team assigned to us at birth. Besides our guardians and loved ones in spirit, that team consists of our guides and ancestors. Our guides are energies who may or may not have lived a human life before, but their purpose is to help us navigate our journey on earth. Guides love using angel numbers to communicate with us. Let's say you're going through a difficult time and constantly see the number 555. When you look up its meaning, you see that your guides are telling you that although you're in a time of upheaval, better days are ahead. Sometimes, receiving a simple message of reassurance is all you need to keep moving forward.

Ancestors will also hop on the angel number train and send you well wishes and messages. Your ancestors are those family members you may have never known while they lived on earth, yet who still watch out for you. Maybe you're about to graduate college, as the first person to do so in your family. What you do in this life helps heal your ancestral line, backward and forward in time. So, for a few months before graduation, you may see 3333 everywhere. The message attached to 3333 is that of breaking generational patterns. This is your ancestors' way of communicating that you've become a positive influence within the family, and they're very proud.

Now that you know who sends these messages you need to be aware of all the ways in which you can receive these important communications.

CHAPTER 3

WAYS TO RECEIVE ANGEL NUMBERS

COMMUNICATION WITH ANGELS is mind-blowing. What's particularly amazing about it is how the messages can come from the simplest or most unassuming places. In our purest form, we are Spirit in a limitless form, but as humans, we come with plenty of limits. The wonder is that angels know this and work within our limits to get us the messages we need.

So, what are some of the ways we receive angel numbers? Let's start with an easy one—dreams. How many times have you had a dream in which you saw a number repeatedly? Maybe it prompted you to get up the next day and play that number in the lotto or simply wonder about its importance. Our dreams are an excellent place to receive messages because that is when and where we're most relaxed. It's a great receptive state. We're dealing in the subconscious when asleep and allowed to visit the in-between, the space between our world and the next. Many times our spirit team sends us messages there. An excellent way to begin working with your angels to receive more angel number messages is to keep a dream journal. This can be a physical journal you keep near your bed or an open page in the notes section of your phone. The more you work with dreams, the more you will remember and retain of them. If you're worried this won't work because you never remember your dreams, simply setting the intention to recall them can change that. Before going to bed each night, state aloud or within your mind that you'd like to receive a message in the form of angel numbers. Ask your angels to help you remember upon waking, so you can recall the numbers you saw. Make this a practice, and you'll be amazed at how much information you'll receive from your dreams.

Okay, maybe dreams seem the obvious route to receive angel numbers. Are there other ways? Yes, loads! The intelligence of Spirit is always illustrated brilliantly in the ways in which they communicate with us. For example, what is the number one thing many of us engage in these days? Be honest. Binging our favorite shows, right? That's actually an excellent way for your angels to get you the messages you need. When you're watching your favorite hottie in that series everyone's talking about, do any numbers pop out at you? Besides the main character's six-pack, of course. Does a certain number stick out to you in the dialogue? Did a series of numbers repeat that only you seemed to notice? Your angels get their point across, but they're subtle about it. Pay attention when listening to music or podcasts, or reading your favorite book. Actually, anytime you're relaxing and not really thinking is a perfect time to receive a message. Idle minds are very receptive to new information.

Beyond dreams and media, angel numbers can reach us other ways. Almost anywhere you come into contact with numbers has the potential to bring a message with it. One of my favorite ways to confirm or validate an angel number message is to see the same number in many different forms. For example, I bought breakfast that cost $7.77. Later in the day, I noticed a popular video I was watching had 777 comments. Then, on the news that night, a story reported 777 chickens got loose when a semitruck carrying them overturned. At this point, I realized my angels were trying desperately to send me a message.

Although angel numbers are real, it's always good to keep your objectivity intact. If you see an angel number once and without much else to confirm it's a message, it's only a number. When you see a number repeatedly, at least three separate times within a period of a few days, that's an angel number. And once you do decipher an angel number's meaning, you likely won't see the number again until your angels need to send you a similar message in the future.

CHAPTER 4

ANGEL NUMBER GLOSSARY

IN THIS BOOK, angel numbers are categorized for ease of use and classification. They are divided into base, master, repeating, sequential, patterned, and personal numbers. Angel numbers will range from single to quadruple digits. For each number, keywords, meanings, an affirmation, and activation are given. There are a few meanings listed for every entry. This is a prime example of the intelligence of Spirit. As is frequently found within the English language, one word can have several meanings. This is true for angel numbers as well, so you can receive the right message at the right time.

Let's say you encounter the number 111 repeatedly right before starting a new business. As one of its meanings is new beginnings, this message makes perfect sense. However, later in your life you find yourself at a crossroads, and your angels send 111 once again. In this different situation, you now resonate with another key meaning of 111, transformation. Use your discernment to know which message your angels are sending. It will always make sense and offer insight regarding your current situation.

Besides the meanings of each number, an affirmation and activation are listed. The affirmation allows you to reflect on the energy of the angel number, whereas the activation lets you take it a step further and hone that energy in a proactive way. This takes your interaction with your angels from passive to active. For example, it's reassuring to hear that help is on the way, but it's even better when you can take steps to ensure it shows up as quickly as possible.

Although no psychic ability is required to communicate with your angels, learning how to decipher their messages is a great exercise in building and honing your intuition. Learn what the messages mean, and pay attention to how that information affects you. Do you get goosebumps or chills when you hear a message that resonates? Does your stomach get butterflies? Does your face flush? Your body will help confirm when the message rings true. The more you trust those intuitive hits in your body, the stronger that instinct will become.

BASE NUMBERS

To understand the messages being sent to you, you must have a foundation, a base, from which to build the interpretation. That's what base numbers are. The base numbers are the single digits 1–9. Each individual number has its own unique energy and frequency. All other numbers in this book will build upon these base digits. You will find some of the activations employ reducing an angel number to its single-digit root to harness its base number's strength. This is accomplished by adding together each numeral within an angel number until only a single digit is left. For example, angel number 12 can reduce to 3 by adding 1 + 2. This is helpful when working with large angel numbers to distill them into their foundational essence. Before getting started, a note about the number 0. Zero, by very definition, represents no quantity. It is used as a placeholder without value. For this reason, this number is not traditionally found in angel numbers.

Keywords: independence, fearlessness, step out on your own

Meanings: It's said that one is the loneliest number, but it's actually the most independent and strongest. If you're seeing 1 many times over, it's time to revel in your self-worth and identity and give the world a look at what you offer. Your angels are supporting you as you're ready to spread your wings and fly. Maybe you've been toying with the idea of starting a business or going back to school. Perhaps you're in a relationship, but you have doubts about your partner's commitment. This angel number's message is all about making yourself a priority. Know that you have all you need to strike out on your own. There's no better time to bet on yourself than now. Don't hesitate. Be fearless and take that leap of faith.

Affirmation: It's time to take a step out on my own.

Activation: As you begin any new project, take a yellow string and tie one knot in it. Recite the affirmation over it and place it somewhere on the right side of your body. Carry it until your new venture is up and running. This will boost your confidence and ensure success.

Keywords: decision time, balance needed, keep the faith

Meanings: This or that? Which path should I take? Have these types of questions been on your mind lately? Possibly, if you're seeing this angel number. Your angels want you to know it's time to make a choice. Once you do, life gets moving again. Sometimes, we spend so much time trying to make a choice that we end up slowing our progress in the process. This message is also about finding balance. Maybe you're juggling a couple of jobs or too many responsibilities and, so, are feeling stressed. Your guardian spirits send this message as a gentle reminder to find some stability and reprioritize. This angel number also tells you to keep believing in what you're doing. Although the path may be difficult at the moment, have faith it will be worth it.

Affirmation: I welcome more balance into my life.

Activation: Find two equally sized objects and hold them in your hands. Set a timer for two minutes. During that time, close your eyes and ask silently for stability over any areas in your life that feel off-kilter. When the timer goes off, offer gratitude for the help. Do this any time you feel the need for balance.

Keywords: communication, speak your truth, change it up

Meanings: You have the floor—it's time to speak up. When this angel number enters your life, it brings a message of communication. It's often said that three's a crowd, but you need a crowd to be heard. What good does it do to speak your truth only to yourself? Your angels are urging you to open up and let your voice be heard. If you've been putting off a difficult conversation or feel as though you're about to burst if you don't let something out, it's most likely the reason you're seeing this number. This angel number also shows up when there's stagnation in your life. You're being encouraged to switch up your routine or try something different to break up the monotony.

Affirmation: I honor myself by speaking my truth.

Activation: There are several chakras, or energy centers, throughout the body, but the one connected with your ability to communicate is located near the throat. When you aren't able to express yourself or speak your truth, your throat chakra can suffer. So, let's clear that chakra and strengthen your ability to speak up. Choose a location where you can speak loudly, such as your backyard, bedroom, or garage. Clear your throat and shout, "This is my voice. This is my truth. I will be heard." Say it at least three times until you truly feel it. You should feel a release within your body, most likely around your throat or shoulders, but anywhere you feel a weight lifted means you've accomplished the task of making yourself heard.

Keywords: restored balance, keep going, pay attention to detail

Meanings: Four is a symbol of stability. Think of a standard chair. Four legs carry the weight of the seat's load equally. So, this number brings news that stability is being restored to your life. Maybe you've been feeling overwhelmed with too many tasks or with life in general. You can breathe a sigh of relief as things will be sorted out for you. You may receive help in the form of others coming to your aid or receiving monetary resources. As numbers progress, they represent a new level attained. Four represents reaching almost midpoint. So, things may feel shaky and uncertain, but your guardians want you to keep going. They stand with you on your journey. This angel number also reminds you to be mindful of the little things. The devil's in the details. So, if you find something not going according to plan, be sure to dot your "I"s and cross your "T"s to manage the issue.

Affirmation: I will keep moving forward on my journey.

Activation: On a piece of paper, draw four 4s in the shape of a square with a 4 in each corner. Fold the paper four times, each time toward you. Carry this with you whenever you feel unbalanced, need motivation, or want to be more focused on the task at hand.

Keywords: transition period, fast-paced changes, need for freedom

Meanings: In the middle of any journey, you face that uncertain bit, the transition period. You've come far enough not to turn back, but still have a distance to go before reaching the finish line. When you see the number 5, you're most likely in that murky area of life, but your angels want you to remember it's temporary. Soon, you'll be moving into more stable and enjoyable territory. This message will also find you when many situations in life are changing all at once. Take a breath. Things will slow down soon. When you're feeling held back or hemmed in, your angels will also send this number to urge you to free yourself by taking a different path.

Affirmation: I embrace change, as it helps me learn and grow.

Activation: Draw a star with five points. Next to each of the five points, write down an area of life, such as finances, love, health, etc., that you need help with. Once completed, one at a time, focus your mind on each area. After you've finished, place the star beneath a blue, orange, or yellow candle and light the candle. As it burns, it releases your intention of being open to change in your life to the Universe, and that your angels can help work out the details. **Note:** Never leave burning candles or any fire unattended. If you cannot complete a ritual in one sitting, snuff the candle out and simply relight it as soon as you're able. Please don't blow the candle out as that disperses the energy, requiring you to start over from the beginning.

Keywords: peace after a turbulent time, starting a family, service to others

Meanings: If you've been going through a rough patch, your angels want you to know that those times are ending. They're sending you comfort and reassurance after times of hardship, particularly those kinds that steal your peace of mind, such as financial difficulties or dysfunctional family dynamics. The great news is, soon peace will be restored. This angel number also means it's a good time to add to your family, if you've been considering it. Countless times, my clients have shared that, in the days and weeks leading up to learning of their pregnancy or adoption going through, they were inundated with the number 6. It's your angels' way of saying, "There's a new bundle of joy on the way!" You may also receive this number if you've been thinking of or recently started doing community service or charity work. Your guardian spirits are affirming that this activity will be rewarding for you and those you'll be serving.

Affirmation: Peace is being restored to my life.

Activation: For six days in a row, wake up each day and, before doing anything else, simply state, "I am so grateful for the peace in my life." On the sixth and final day, once you've made the statement, clap your hands six times. Then, with hands in prayer position over your heart, feel serenity entering your heart space. There may be a warm sensation or tingling in this area. This exercise helps you become more aware of the peace you already experience as well as invite more into your life.

Keywords: luck is turning, mysticism, detachment

Meanings: Seven is abuzz with the frequency of luck. If you're seeing this number frequently, your luck will be turning very soon. Perhaps nothing has gone your way recently. Fear not, as your angels want you to know those days are moving behind you. Also, when this number finds you, you may feel drawn to the metaphysical arts. Maybe you're questioning whether they're for you. Have you been interested in crystals, tarot, or other spiritual practices? Your angels are encouraging you to delve deep and learn more. Angel number 7 also vibrates with the frequency of detachment. Don't worry. Your angels aren't asking you to become emotionless. They simply want you to let go of expectations. Do things from your heart without worrying about success or failure.

Affirmation: I will work on letting go of expectations.

Activation: Each day for a week, on a small piece of paper, write down something you want to bring into your life. It can be anything from money to better health to romance. Stack each subsequent piece of paper on top of the previous one. On the last day, take the stack, which contains seven different things you want to manifest, and place it in a firesafe container, such as a grill or fire pit. Then, light the paper and let it burn completely (do not leave it unattended). Once completely cool, dispose of any ashes in the trash. This releases your desires into the universe for manifestation, with an extra boost of luck, and allows you to practice detaching from what will happen. Simply have faith that it will.

Keywords: unexpected financial gain, infinite potential, true love

Meanings: This is an extremely good number to see! Seeing angel number 8 frequently means you will soon have a surprise monetary gain. A winning lottery ticket or unexpected refund may be headed your way. It's also a message from your guardian spirits that your potential is limitless. Maybe you've been doubting your ability to accomplish a task or goal, and you're repeatedly bombarded by the number 8. Your angels are reminding you that you're an infinite soul having a human experience. You have tons of potential to unlock. Also, when this number finds you repeatedly, true love is headed your way. This can be either a confirmation that the relationship you're in is the real deal or that someone truly special will enter your life.

Affirmation: I'm a limitless being with endless potential.

Activation: To call abundance into your life using the number 8, try this easy exercise. Find a playing card with an 8 on it, such as the eight of spades, a tarot card, like the eight of pentacles, or simply draw one yourself. Take this card and place it in your wallet or purse. Carry it with you at all times to be financially blessed.

Keywords: expertise, time to lead, helping others

Meanings: As the last of the single-digit angel numbers, 9 comes with messages of proficiency and leadership. As the numbers increased, lessons and experiences have been learned and earned. So, your angels will use this number to let you know you've reached a level of expertise, and it's time for you to demonstrate it. This might mean you take that step out on faith to start your own business. Many times, this number is sent because you're being called to lead, such as with a promotion at work or a chance for you to head a passion project. You will also see this angel number when you're able to help others. Do you have skills that others could benefit from? Have you ever thought of teaching? Your angels want you to consider using your abilities to assist others.

Affirmation: I'm ready to step up and lead.

Activation: To be recognized for your expertise and leadership qualities, try this. Get either a jasper, red coral, or sapphire crystal. Deep red and blue resonate with the energy of the angel number 9. Wear one of these stones in a piece of jewelry, or simply carry it in your pocket. This will increase your magnetism, enticing those in positions of power to recognize your skills and worth.

MASTER NUMBERS

As you've seen, each number plays an important role in our lives, complete with its own frequency and vibration. However, there is a group of angel numbers that carries a little extra power and more oomph than the rest. These numbers carry special messages and lessons that we have to work to incorporate into our lives, or master, if you will. That's why we refer to these as master numbers. The special energy of these double digits holds a powerful message for you, and they appear at pivotal life moments.

Keywords: spiritual awakening, soulmate potential, partnerships

Meanings: Your angels have something powerful to share with you. Many times, when someone begins to experience symptoms of a spiritual awakening, this angel number appears. A spiritual awakening is a discovery of self that makes you question almost everything you think you know about the world. As this can be a difficult time, your angels want you to know they're with you on the journey. This angel number also appears when a soulmate may enter your life. Perhaps you've been thinking of your current partner as the one, but you'd like to be sure. Seeing 11 over and over is a validation that you've met that certain someone. You could also be receiving an opportunity to partner with someone in a business sense. Maybe you're looking for a partner with whom to start a podcast or YouTube channel. This is your angels' way of letting you know it's definitely possible.

Affirmation: I am ready to walk my spiritual path.

Activation: Spiritual awakenings can be disorienting, so it's important to center yourself. One of the best ways to do that is through meditation. You can start with one minute at a time. Be patient with yourself as it takes practice to get into the groove. The trick is not to remove all thoughts from your mind, because that's impossible, but instead to acknowledge the thoughts as they come, then watch them go. Through consistency, meditation can still your mind and bring you peace, even in the most chaotic times.

Keywords: dreams, the right decision, push ahead

Meanings: Your angels are telling you to pay special attention to your dreams. Important information, and even visitations with loved ones in spirit, are possible at this time. Upon waking, jot down whatever you can remember of your dreams. The more you do this, the more you will remember. Also, you may see this angel number when you're worrying over a decision you've recently made. Stop fretting right now—your angels say you've made the right decision. Embrace your choice and move forward. Perhaps you find yourself in a state of frozen animation. You're bogged down by responsibilities. It's possible you feel like giving up. Your angels are asking you to hold tight and push ahead when they send this angel number. Although there may be struggle at the moment, your guardian spirits are always by your side.

Affirmation: I'm secure in the decisions I've made.

Activation: Before bed, place a small piece of lapis lazuli, clear quartz, or amethyst under your pillow. Any of these three crystals can help enhance dreams, increasing the likelihood of having more insightful and lucid dreams as well as making them easier to decipher. Again, upon waking, write down whatever you remember. Many important messages can be sent through dreams.

Keywords: master teacher guide, feeling inspired, new insights

Meanings: When 33 seems to be chasing you everywhere you go, you have a new guide entering your life, and not just any guide, but a master teacher. A master teacher is an ascended guide who lived a life on earth but fit a divine archetype, such as Buddha, Jesus, Krishna, Mother Mary, etc. For this unique and divine soul to start working with you means you're taking a big step forward on your life's journey and fulfilling your divine purpose. This number may also appear because you'll be receiving a boost of inspiration. You may find your creativity is off the charts. Your angels are with you, and they're happy to inspire you by bringing even more ideas. Also, if you've been trying to solve a problem for a while but can't seem to work it out, your angels want you to know an answer is coming. Something you've never thought of could strike and help you find a solution for that issue you've been puzzling over.

Affirmation: My creativity is divinely inspired.

Activation: If you'd like a stronger connection to any of the master teachers, find a small statue of them and place it on your altar, end table, or whatever space you use for spiritual worship. Speak to the statue daily, place your prayers beneath it, and allow it to represent your connection to those higher powers interceding on your behalf.

Keywords: others support you, double-check plans, determination will pay off

Meanings: When seeing the angel number 44, your ideas will be supported by others. Maybe you've been hesitant to mention plans to friends and family about going back to school or starting an Etsy account. Maybe you're writing your great American novel but are worried that no one will read it. Your angels want you to know to keep pursuing those goals because you have more support than you realize. Also, when you see 44, you're receiving a gentle reminder to reassess current plans to keep things moving smoothly. It's possible that your particular situation finds you knee-deep in an existing project, but you're unsure whether it's going to work out. Your angels send this number so you know that your grit and determination will pay off in the long run. Don't doubt your drive.

Affirmation: My persistence will pay off.

Activation: Whenever you feel your willpower waning, try this simple technique to boost it. Deep purple resonates with the energy of 44. Find a candle in this color, a piece of felt, or even a favorite T-shirt. Wear that T-shirt whenever you need an extra lift in spirit to keep going. Carry the felt somewhere on your person to channel that energy. Light the candle and meditate in front of it to hone that supportive angel number 44 energy.

Keywords: congratulations on making changes,
releasing regrets, time to travel

Meanings: You must have made some recent changes in your life that have improved your situation because, when you see 55, your angels are sending congratulations. Your angels have seen what you've done, and they're so proud of you. Also, the energy of angel number 55 lets you know that your angels want you to release regrets. Five's energy is all about being in the thick of it. It comes having just started something, but before it's finally over. If you know you've been carrying around a burden for far too long, now's an excellent time to put it down. This angel number also appears when you're ready to travel. Your angels are all for it. Put on your vacation clothes, and strike out for a little rest and relaxation. You've earned it!

Affirmation: I'm so proud of my progress.

Activation: To embrace the angel number 55, take a little time off. This can be just a weekend getaway or a month-long stay in Bali. Carry the number 55 as either a charm on a necklace or on a piece of paper on your person. It will increase the fun and spontaneity of your trip.

Keywords: mother wound healing, clairvoyance, harmony restored

Meanings: Your angels love to use this number to point out it's time to heal your mother wound. The mother wound is intergenerational trauma passed down through your family's maternal line. Healing this can take the form of starting therapy or simply acknowledging that you have a mother wound to heal. Your angels will support you in this effort. Another reason you see this number is that you're about to have a psychic skill blossom, namely clairvoyance. Clear seeing, or clairvoyance, is a psychic sense that allows you to receive information through visual images within your mind's eye. Call on your angels to help you hone this skill. If you've been dealing with strife and anxiety, your angels will also send this number to let you know harmony is being restored. Keep your spirits up. Better times are ahead.

Affirmation: Harmony has been restored to my life.

Activation: To strengthen your clairvoyance, try these simple exercises. One of the easiest ways to begin using your clairvoyance is by tapping into your imagination. Make a list of items, then picture them in your mind, one by one. Once you can accomplish that, move on to blindfolding yourself and guessing images on cards. You may want to have a partner for this. The more you work on it, the stronger your clairvoyance will become.

Keywords: in tune with nature, finding your spiritual path, stepping into your power

Meanings: Your guides are asking you to take some time out in nature. It's likely you've felt unbalanced or a little out of control. Nothing settles your soul more than spending time with Mother Nature. You can accomplish this by going to the beach, hiking in the mountains, or taking an easy stroll in the park. Seeing this angel number also means you're finding your spiritual path. Possibly, you've been thinking about taking up a meditation practice or learning tarot or Reiki. This is confirmation to continue down that path. Also, your angels may be trying to tell you to step into your power now. That could be accomplished by taking a leadership position at work or making sure your voice is being heard. Stepping into your power can also refer to you fully owning who you are and all you're capable of.

Affirmation: I'm in my element within nature.

Activation: Whether you'd like to increase your connection to nature or heighten your spiritual connection, both can be accomplished through grounding. Grounding is the practice of balancing your energy through earth's vibrations by walking barefoot outside, sitting among trees, or simply being in nature. Do this to help strengthen your bond with Mother Nature, but also to remember your place within the natural order of the world, thus putting you more in touch with your spiritual side.

88

Keywords: recognized for achievement, money coming in, possible psychic visions

Meanings: Get excited when you receive this angel number because you'll soon be recognized for a great achievement. This could be in the form of a raise or promotion at work or winning an award for something you're a part of. Whatever form it takes, your angels are very happy for you. Seeing 88 several times is also an alert that you have money coming, and it can come in many forms. Maybe your TikTok account is taking off. Brand deals are trickling in. You're getting more business than ever before. Each of these areas represents a possible revenue stream. Seeing 88 also signals potential psychic visions. The double 8s resonate with the energy of heightened psychic abilities. Visions are another way for your angels to communicate with you.

Affirmation: Money flows to me effortlessly.

Activation: To enhance the energy of angel number 88 and call more money into your life, try this simple exercise. Get a green tapered candle, as green represents money. Carve into the candle four dollar signs and two 88s. Place this on your bedside table or altar. No need to light it. It simply represents a focal point for the abundance to find you. Every day, or at least each time you can, place your loose change at the base of the candle. As the change adds up so, too, will the money in your life.

Keywords: natural lightworker, lending your experience, energetic downloads

Meanings: This is a spiritually charged angel number. Chances are you're a natural lightworker, someone pulled to work toward the betterment of humanity, helping raise the collective consciousness. If this resonates with your life experiences, your angels are letting you know to step into that role. Also, this number encourages you to lend your experience to teach others. Are you an excellent pianist? Can you crochet anything under the sun? Think about taking your skills to the masses. Your angels are saying, "Do it!" You may also receive some energetic downloads when seeing this number frequently. Downloads are spiritual insights that bring profound thoughts and raise your vibration.

Affirmation: My experience can help others.

Activation: Since 99 is a deeply spiritual number, you can channel its energy to bring many spiritual gifts to your life. Use it during meditation. You can focus on the number in your mind. You can chant it. You can write it on a piece of paper and hold that between your palms while focusing on strengthening your spiritual gifts. Also, 99 resonates with the color white for its purity. Dress in this color when meditating or performing spiritual activities to heighten the energy.

REPEATING NUMBERS

Three- and four-digit number combinations that consist of the same number are called repeating angel numbers. Since the same number repeats, the strength of that number increases with each addition. This enhances the power of the message as well. This is why most people think of angel numbers only in the scope of three- and four-digit numbers: because they hold such important meanings.

111

Keywords: transformation, triple blessings, new beginnings

Meanings: You're going through a transformation when you receive this angel number. A transformation is a new phase of life that changes everything, like a pregnancy, a college acceptance, or even retirement. Your angels send extra love when you go through these crucial life moments. You'll also be sent 111 as a representation of triple blessings in your life. This can be a raise much greater than anticipated. Yes, it could mean you're expecting more than one baby at a time. It doesn't necessarily mean you're receiving exactly three times an amount, but it will certainly feel that way. Also, anytime you find the number 1, there's a message of new beginnings. You're about to embark on a new adventure, and you have your angels firmly by your side.

Affirmation: May blessings flow into my life.

Activation: Who doesn't want to experience more blessings in their life? Since 111 signifies triple blessings, try this to enhance that energy. Maybe you'd like a raise or to win a scratch-off lottery ticket three times the normal amount. Take any intention you want to manifest and write it on a piece of paper three times in a vertical row. Then, dab the paper with success oil, which you can either buy through a botanica or create your own by mixing jojoba oil with a pinch of sandalwood, frankincense, and bay leaf essential oils. Carry this paper with you whenever you need that extra boost of success.

Keywords: comfort zone, karmic cycle ending, answered prayers

Meanings: Don't stop now! Your angels want you to go beyond your comfort zone. Get out of your own way and push back on those fears. Everything you've been wanting is just beyond that area of stability and comfort. Also, your angels may be letting you know a karmic cycle has ended. This is welcomed news if you've been struggling through a particularly difficult situation. Once you've learned of and fulfilled karmic debts, new roads and paths always open. This is also a message letting you know that not only have your prayers been heard, but they've also been answered. If you've been losing sleep or worrying long hours over an issue out of your control, let this be reassurance that it's all coming to an end.

Affirmation: Beyond my comfort zone is where my next adventure lies.

Activation: Rose quartz is a crystal that resonates with the energy of 222. It embodies unconditional support and love, especially for yourself. When you're in a situation where a karmic cycle has ended, or you're stepping out of your comfort zone, carry this stone for support. You can also place it beneath your pillow while you sleep. This will serve as a channel for your angels to send you very high-frequency vibrations, bringing you clarity, peace, and joy.

Keywords: express yourself, assess relationships, releasing negativity

Meanings: Your angels are ready for you to let loose! When you see this message, you're being asked to express yourself. Whether it's writing, singing, drawing, or any other form of expression, it's time to share your gifts with the world. You can also receive this number if it's time to take stock of your relationships. Has a friendship gone sour? Is there someone overstepping your boundaries? Take a close look at these situations and make changes, if necessary. Releasing negativity is also an important message connected with the angel number 333. You may need to let go of anger toward certain people or situations, or cut ties with negative people in your circle. Either way, it's time to raise your vibes.

Affirmation: I release any negative emotions, people, and situations from my life.

Activation: Buy a black candle because black absorbs and removes negativity and fears. Carve into the candle anything you want to rid yourself of. For example, you can write "anxiety," "stress," "fear," "negativity," etc. Then, light the candle, and as it burns, those issues will be lifted and lessened in your life. Watch the smoke. The darker it turns, the stronger the result. Remember to never leave candles unattended.

Keywords: try again, divinely protected, take a class

Meanings: If you've given up a certain hobby or career because of earlier disappointments or failures, your spirit team is encouraging you to try again. It's not too late to fulfill your dreams. Sometimes, you have to go through failure to learn what not to do in the future. You might also be receiving a message of divine protection. Perhaps you've been involved in an abusive relationship, or you simply fear the situation you find yourself in. Your angels want you to know that you are divinely protected, and you should seek freedom from the situation. Also, if you've been toying with the idea of taking up a new skill, let this be confirmation to go for it. Your angels always support you in endeavors that stretch you. Sign up for a class today!

Affirmation: I am divinely protected.

Activation: To hone the energy of angel number 444 and feel closer to that divine protection, purchase an angel statue. Place it on your altar or near where you sleep. Having a physical representation of a guardian angel gives you a sense of peace, calm, and protection.

Keywords: upheaval, surrender to the moment, better days ahead

Meanings: This angel number represents a time of upheaval. Though life may be chaotic right now, your angels send this message to let you know they're with you and will never leave your side. You're not alone while going through tough times. You will always be guided, especially when it's dark. This message also comes to tell you to surrender to what's happening. Sometimes, the harder we fight, the worse it gets. When something is for your higher purpose, it's easier to be in flow with it and trust things will work out. Your angels also want you to know, particularly when times are hard, that better days are ahead. Keep the faith.

Affirmation: I trust that all things are working in my favor.

Activation: Whenever life becomes overwhelming, try this technique for a better perspective on things. Take a sheet of paper and divide it into three columns, each with a 5 at the top. Under the first column, write down five issues you're struggling with. Beneath the second column, write down five things you're grateful for, and in the third column, write down five ways your issues can be resolved in your favor. This allows your mind to see solutions instead of problems.

Keywords: nothing to fear, refocus your energy, time for self-care

Meanings: This angel number has gotten a bad rap. It has nothing to do with evil. It's actually a number that your angels use to let you know there's nothing to fear. Perhaps you've been overburdened with worries or having nightmares. Your angels want to reassure you that you need not be afraid. This angel number also comes to you signifying a great time to refocus your energy. Instead of thinking about what you can't do or the limitations you face, think of what you can accomplish. Also, your angels are encouraging you to take time for yourself. Make sure to practice some self-care, especially when stressed, to help alleviate the strain. Go to the salon, meditate, hydrate, get a massage, or get out of town for a few days. Do something that will lift your spirits.

Affirmation: I have nothing to fear.

Activation: Here's an easy way to reclaim the energy of this number from the negative, back to its original positive intent. Anytime you see the number 666, state in your mind, "I have nothing to fear. My angels are always near."

Keywords: incredibly lucky, momentum, magnetic

Meanings: Is everything going your way right now? That's because you're extremely lucky at the moment, and your angels want to bring your attention to it. Press your luck a little as things are most likely to work out in your favor. If you're not yet feeling extra lucky, things are about to turn around in a big way. You will also see this angel number when you've been muddling along and feeling sluggish. Momentum will soon pick up. So, if you dig deep and push, you'll see things start to move. Your angels also love to send this number when you're about to become the center of attention. Your magnetism is high. You could launch a website, podcast, or business now, and it's sure to be successful.

Affirmation: I'm a magnet for luck, health, and abundance.

Activation: To extend your extremely lucky season, wear a piece of jewelry with the number 7 as a charm; even better if there are three 7s. Also, write 777 on a slip of paper and place it in your right shoe, so your luck walks everywhere you do.

Keywords: Midas touch, healing generational wealth, abundance

Meanings: Does everything you touch seem to turn to gold? Or are you hoping it will? When seeing the number 888, if you're not already experiencing it, you will very soon have the Midas touch. So, everything you start in this season will be out-of-this-world prosperous. Many times, you receive this message because you're healing generational wealth wounds for your family. You've learned how to tend to your money. You've learned that money represents energy. You've become a saver or made money moves your parents or grandparents couldn't even fathom. The work you're doing is important because it not only helps the generations after you, but it also affects the generations who came before. With the triple 8s, your angels also want to remind you that abundance is available for you. Enjoy the overflow!

Affirmation: My healthy relationship with money heals generational wounds.

Activation: More money is always nice to have. To channel the abundance of 888, make a honey jar. Find a Mason jar; any size will do. Before filling it, either place stickers of the number 8 on the outside of the jar, or use a permanent marker to write the number 8 on the glass. Then, write 888 on paper, fold it eight times, place it in the jar, and fill the jar with honey. Keep this near a window so the sun can warm it each day to keep your relationship flowing like honey—sweet, golden, and delicious.

999

Meanings: Your angels are asking you to step into your authenticity at this time. Maybe you've picked up habits or acquaintances that don't speak to your higher purpose. Usually, when you receive this angel number, you're aware that you haven't been living in the most authentic ways. This is a gentle reminder from your angels to get back on track. When 999 pops up everywhere, don't be surprised to find yourself crying a lot as well—you're experiencing an emotional release. Let those tears flow as they help wash away trapped trauma and energy within your aura. You may also experience some soul growth when 999 finds you. Your angels bring this to your attention to let you know you're not going through a hard time or struggling at the moment for no reason. The situations you're dealing with will help you grow. Call on them anytime you feel overwhelmed during this time.

Affirmation: I strive to live as my most authentic self.

Activation: Selenite is a crystal that helps remove anything from your auric energy field that doesn't belong to you. To step into your most authentic self, carry a piece of selenite with you, wear a piece of selenite jewelry, or sleep with it under your pillow.

1111

Keywords: manifesting portal, make amends, once-in-a-lifetime opportunity

Meanings: If you're not familiar with any other angel number, you most likely know this one. It is known as the wishing angel number because, whenever you see it, it's time to make a wish. This makes it the perfect manifesting portal. When your angels send this number to you, a manifesting portal has opened in your life. You can now draw in what you want faster than ever before. You may also be receiving this number as encouragement to repair relationships. Maybe you had a falling out with a friend or argument with a loved one. Your angels have a higher perspective. They can see when the timing is good to make amends. You may also have a unique opportunity coming into your life with this angel number. This can be a trip to a distant place or a job offer you never thought you'd get. Say "yes" to the Universe when this chance comes your way.

Affirmation: I welcome unique opportunities.

Activation: Anytime you see 1111 is a great time to make your intentions known to the Universe. As stated earlier, when you see 1111, make a wish. This number resonates with the energy of 1, which is all about new beginnings. It opens a portal that speeds manifesting. So, anytime you see the number 1111, send your intentions into the universe because the Universe is listening and ready to make your dreams come true.

Keywords: love and devotion, right place at the right time, heaviness lifting

Meanings: Overwhelming love and devotion are headed your way. If you're in an established relationship, you may feel recharged and refreshed in your love for one another. If you're single, a partner who deserves you is on the way. Your angels will send this message to let you know you're in the right place at the right time. The angel number 2222 is also associated with a deep heaviness lifting from your life. You may have a breakthrough in a therapy session or a really good cry with a friend that leaves you feeling lighter and brighter, opening up new pathways for your future as you heal.

Affirmation: With divine timing, everything happens at exactly the right moment.

Activation: Take four yellow candles and divide them into two pair. On the left, those two candles represent what you'd like removed. On the right, those candles represent what you're calling in. You can carve symbols into each set of candles to represent what you want to let go of and call in, or write it on a piece of paper and place the paper before each pair. Light the candles and let them burn in two-hour segments (never leave burning candles unattended) until they burn all the way down. Take the melted wax and paper that remains (if any) and dispose of it by tossing it into the trash over your left shoulder for what's being removed, and over your right shoulder for what you are calling in.

Keywords: breaking generational patterns,
succeeding against all odds, work your magic

Meanings: You hold a special spot in your family when your angels send this message. As many have come to understand, what happened in the past affects us still today, with many of those issues starting in our families. There are those among us who were sent here to stop these cycles from continuing. You are being acknowledged as one of them. Your angels want to make you aware of your higher purpose. They know how hard this can be and are so proud of you. Also, the message from your angels could be that you'll get through whatever you're currently facing, even if it seems insurmountable. Miracles happen every day. This message is meant to remind you of that. If you're someone who works magic, such as healing rituals, spellwork, etc., your angels are letting you know that now is an excellent time to do so. The angel number 3333 resonates with the frequency of higher-intentioned actions. When your magic comes from the heart, it's bound to succeed.

Affirmation: It is in the darkest hour that my light shines brightest.

Activation: Before or after working magic, or if you simply need a spiritual cleansing, take a spiritual bath (because this bath is for spiritual purposes, cleanse yourself in a separate shower beforehand). Fill your bath with water and add dried lavender, chamomile, and calendula in heaping handfuls. Sit in the bath and allow the water to soothe and cleanse you. Before draining the tub, save a bowl full of water and toss it outside, signifying your cleansing ritual is complete.

Keywords: inspiring others, devotion, past-life cycle

Meanings: Your angels want you to know that your life is motivational to others. Take this as a sign to start a career in service or share your life story with others, possibly in the form of a book or podcast. Don't dismiss your experiences as mundane. You can be a light for others. This message also finds you if your faith has been waning. Now is not the time to give up. Hang in there because your angels know you've been having a hard time; things will ease soon. Stay devoted to your path. This message is also sent to notify you that a past-life cycle that came into this life with you has ended. You have met your karmic debt and are now free of that lesson. You may find certain patterns that have always plagued you are no longer an issue.

Affirmation: I'm grateful for the past-life lessons I've learned.

Activation: Try this meditation to make peace with a past-life cycle. Sit or lie in a quiet area. With eyes closed, use the angel number 4444 as a portal to your past lives. Ask your angels to come close and help you make peace with those past-life lessons. Imagine a blue 4444 glowing in your mind. Ask your past-life lesson to step forward. The number will begin to twist and turn, slowly forming into other images, which will tap you into that karmic debt. Send love to those issues. Before opening your eyes, offer gratitude for the lesson as it's now firmly behind you.

Keywords: rise like a phoenix, renovate and renew, see how far you've come

Meanings: Life has, most likely, been tough lately if your angels are sending this message. However, they want to reassure you that you're about to come back better than ever. Hang tough because your angels haven't left your side and are cheering on your comeback. Your angels may also send this number if it's time to renovate your home, your fashion, your hair, or simply your energy. Fives are always about change. Renew and refresh is the message when you see this number. Also, your angels want to encourage you to take a look back to realize how far you've come. You're still on your journey. To stay motivated, it's good to see how much you've already overcome.

Affirmation: My feathers may be singed, but still I soar.

Activation: Fire can be cleansing and healing. To hasten your rise from the proverbial ashes into your full phoenix glory, try this. Write down five things that have been holding you back and that you'd like to improve or remove from your life. Burn the paper completely. Dig a small hole in the earth, safely where you can and always with permission, and bury those ashes. Alternatively, you can incorporate the ashes into the soil of a potted plant. From that fertile ground, new life will grow, renewing your energy as it does.

6666

Keywords: generational healing, putting yourself first, full heart space

Meanings: Healing is taking place in your family that will affect generations, and you've played a pivotal part in that. It's not an easy role to play, and so your angels commend you. It's also time to put yourself first if your angels have sent this number. You have a big heart for others, but you have to make yourself a priority as well. It's hard to pour from an empty cup. Put your feet up and do something just for you. Your angels also send this number to indicate you're feeling very content in your heart space. Your recent actions and intentions have been particularly heart-driven when you receive this message. Celebrate your growth and enjoy that warm feeling in your heart.

Affirmation: Although not easy, I heal family wounds proudly.

Activation: To strengthen your heart chakra, carry a green aventurine crystal near your heart, either in a pocket, or even a bra or camisole. In meditation, hold the crystal over your chest to increase its effectiveness. This stone is a great healer and protector of your heart chakra energy.

Keywords: trust your instincts, extraterrestrial encounters, transmutation

Meanings: It's time to trust your instincts and go with your gut. Your guides are urging you to listen to your intuition. It won't steer you wrong. In a particularly unique message when you see 7777, your angels will alert you to possible otherworldly encounters. UFO sightings or ghostly apparitions are possible at this time. This signifies that you're open to communication outside of the normal senses. Your angels will also use this number to let you know you can turn your pain into power. Some of the most influential and powerful people in the world have taken their heartbreaks and turned them into breakthroughs. If you feel called to write, vlog, film, or even sing about your experiences, do it. You have the power to transmute these painful circumstances into positive energy.

Affirmation: Every experience is worthwhile, even those that hurt.

Activation: Start an intuition journal. Begin following your gut instincts, those little nudges from the Universe. Document the times things turn out good when you follow those urges. Write about when they don't. The more you practice and dissect through journaling, the more connections you'll see. As a result, your intuition will improve.

8888

Keywords: restoration, spiritual calling, romantic reunion

Meanings: There's restoration happening in your life. It may seem impossible, but your angels are working to return, replace, or restore what's been lost. It's also a message of answering a spiritual calling. Maybe you've felt pulled to serve your faith. Maybe you want to begin reading for people on a psychic level. Your angels have your back and support you in this. Answer that calling. You didn't receive it by chance. This angel number is also shown when there's a romantic reunion on the horizon. Second chances are given every day in matters of the heart. It's possible the one you've missed has been missing you, too.

Affirmation: I'm willing to give love a second try.

Activation: To give someone a second chance, you might try something like this. Use a pink or red prayer candle, a candle traditionally encased in glass for several-day usage. Carve your name and the other person's name into the candle with a needle. Lightly rub the candle with jojoba oil. Then, roll the candle in some rose petals. Dried or fresh will work. Let the candle burn for eight hours. As it burns, think of the person you wish to call back into your life. This will reignite your fire. Again, never leave a burning candle unattended. Snuff it out if you must leave and relight it once you return. Don't blow it out as that scatters the energy and will require you to restart. Ideally, set aside the time needed for your rituals for best results.

9999

Keywords: major transition, integration, next adventure

Meanings: You're at a major transition point in your life. This isn't merely taking a vacation or getting a promotion at work. This is next-level stuff, such as marriage, birth, and rebirth. Seeing this number serves as confirmation that this is a major moment, and your angels are with you every step of the way. Your angels will also send this number if you're going through an integration of information. This can happen when you've had a breakthrough in therapy or an epiphany about life lessons. You have to go through a period of adjustment in which you assimilate this information into your existing belief system. Your angels will guide you through the process. Also, your angels like to give you a heads-up, especially about fun stuff. This is exactly what 9999 represents. You're about to head out on your next adventure. Cross something off of your bucket list or finally do that thing that scares *and* thrills you. Your angels have your back.

Affirmation: I'm ready for my next great adventure.

Activation: As the angel number 9999 can reduce down to its base 9 vibration, you can harness its energy by listening to sounds that resonate at a frequency of 432 Hz. Many free meditation videos and recordings can be found online that include this frequency. Listen whenever you'd like to get ready for the next level in your life or want to prepare for a new adventure.

SEQUENTIAL NUMBERS

Numbers that follow in a consecutive manner, such as 1234, are known as sequential, and can go either in ascending or descending order. Their stair-step effect is what makes them eye-catching and so are a method your angels will use to get your attention and send you messages. This section begins with the ascending sequential numbers followed by the descending sequential numbers.

Keywords: growth, career success, being heard

Meanings: This angel number may seem simple, but when you see it repeatedly it holds a special message. You're going through a period of growth, and your angels are glad to see it. It may not be easy, but they know you will be better for it. This angel number also indicates career success, such as a raise or business expansion. Enjoy the peak, as you've worked through many valleys to stand there. Your angels will also send this number because you're being heard. This can happen when breakthroughs in communication finally occur within families or friendships that have had long-standing issues. Also, if you've been hesitant to speak up, now is the time to communicate. Others will be receptive to hearing you out.

Affirmation: To grow is to change.

Activation: Since 12 can reduce to the number 3, tie three knots in a piece of green yarn or string. As you tie each knot, recite the affirmation. You can hold this string when you meditate to help you through a growth period. You can also carry it in your purse or wallet.

Keywords: unconventional, creativity, follow your heart

Meanings: You are a unique individual when you receive this angel number. Your angels encourage you to continue to march to the beat of a different drummer. They love your unique spirit. The world needs more of it. If you've felt pressured to follow the crowd, fight back with your own beautiful energy. This number is also sent when you need to be more creative. It's easy to get caught up in the daily grind. Bills, diet, kids, work, and more can cause creativity to fall by the wayside, but it's important to tap back into your creative energy to make life worthwhile. This number will also appear when it's time to follow your heart. Stop questioning everyone else about what you should do, and listen to that still, inner voice. You already know the answers. Simply act on them. Your angels will support you.

Affirmation: I'm proud of my individuality.

Activation: To channel spontaneous energy, try this fun and easy exercise. Pick up any book and turn to page 23. Then, find the second paragraph and read the third sentence in it. Let that sentence be a springboard to motivate you to do something fun or, at the very least, let it give you a giggle for the day.

Keywords: extra boost, energy shift, spiritual wisdom

Meanings: You're being sent an extra boost of momentum when you see this angel number. If you've felt stuck or stagnant, this will certainly elevate your spirits. Your angels cannot make decisions or interfere with your life, but they can send a lift from time to time. You may also be feeling an energy shift when this number finds you. Perhaps you've felt in a slump energetically or had a health issue that drained you. Keep your chin up because things are about to get much better. Your angels also want you to trust in the spiritual wisdom you've received. This shows up when you seek help from a spiritual leader or learn about new practices, but then don't accept that what you've learned can help you. This information can be trusted, so be receptive to it.

Affirmation: I'm ready to shift into a new energy.

Activation: To show gratitude and enhance the extra boost your angels are sending, bring an angel into your home. This can be in the form of an angel oracle card, an angel statue, a decorative sign with an angel on it, or an angel aura quartz crystal that resonates with angel energy.

Keywords: new love possible, happiness, open up

Meanings: If you're sent this angel number, especially if you're single, romance is brewing. This is a blessing when you've been searching for a partner. Maybe you've been swiping left for a long time and are ready to swipe right—that is very likely when you see 45 again and again. If you're in a relationship, things may move to the next level. Your angels also send this number when you're soon to experience pure happiness. This energy is joyful and carefree. There will be an extra bounce in your step, and you will feel lighter. This angel number also serves as a reminder to open up emotionally. If you've felt closed off, this is a gentle nudge from your angels to lower your guard. If you want new energy to enter your life, you have to be open to receive it.

Affirmation: My heart is open for new love.

Activation: A simple exercise to infuse your life with more happiness is to bring your favorite color into all aspects of your life. Wear your favorite color in your clothing, buy a car in your favorite color, or paint your house in that color. The color you resonate with is unique to you and helps pull out your happiness.

Keywords: leap of faith, conflict resolution, better health

Meanings: You're being encouraged to take a leap of faith. Your angels know you've been toying with the idea of trying something new, but haven't had the nerve to do it. Step out on faith. Your angels will catch you. Another message tied to this angel number is conflict resolution. Maybe you got caught up in drama at work or in your friend group. Perhaps you have an issue you can't seem to resolve. It's being taken care of for you. Let your angels handle it. This angel number also relays that better health is on the way. Don't put off doctor visits or professional health advice. This is simply an encouragement that things will get better once you address them.

Affirmation: I step out on faith to my next journey.

Activation: At the time of a new moon, try this exercise to start something new. New moons, which represent that first moon phase, are a great time for beginnings. As the moon progresses through its phases, so will the intentions you set at this time. Write them down, speak them aloud, or simply think about what you'd like to bring into your life. Watch your intentions bloom in the coming months.

Keywords: follow your dreams, fresh start, big purchases

Meanings: This is the follow-your-dreams number. Maybe life has slowed your ambitions or issues have popped up that kept you from moving forward. Your angels are lifting you up. Obstacles will clear, and the path will open up to allow you to fly. This angel number also comes with the message of starting fresh. This could come in a relationship, a job, or an educational journey. This is a positive message to receive when things have been slow for a while. This number is also a sign that it's the right time to make a big purchase. You may think that spiritual beings aren't interested in humdrum things like home or car purchases, but they are big parts of our lives, so the angels are there to support them.

Affirmation: I have dreams for a reason, and it's time to follow them.

Activation: When house hunting, do this simple practice to increase your chances of buying the home. If you've found your dream home and can't imagine life without it, recite this as you walk through the home: "To me you belong, no matter where I roam; to you I will come because you're my home." It also helps if you leave a small piece of yourself, like a strand of hair, somewhere on the property to stake your claim to it.

Keywords: dig deep, finding balance, hello from heaven

Meanings: Your angels want you to dig deep and keep pushing. This message usually finds you when you're going through a tough time. Maybe you're contemplating throwing in the towel, but don't do that. Your angels see the bigger picture, and they know if you keep at it you'll achieve your goals. Take a break, if you must, but then get back to it. You'll also see this number when you need to find some balance. All work and no play is a recipe for disaster. If you're overdoing it, take a step back. Conversely, if you're not really doing enough, time to get moving! You can also receive a sweet hello from heaven when this number finds you. If you see this number and a random memory of a loved one pops into your head, or you see something that reminds you of them, chances are, that person is wishing you well and letting you know they're around.

Affirmation: As I dig deep, I know I've got what it takes to make it.

Activation: To encourage more communication with your loved ones in spirit, simply ask. Even if you didn't set up a sign to know it's them before their passing, it's not too late to set one up now. Maybe you notice a particular bird or random animal in your yard. Ask a specific loved one to send that animal around whenever they want to say hello. That way, the next time you see that cardinal or squirrel in your yard, you'll know exactly who sent it.

Keywords: positive communication, forgive yourself, unexpected money

Meanings: You have some good news on the way. Although your angels won't tell you exactly what's coming, you may be able to piece it together from contextual clues. Perhaps you're waiting for news about an offer on a house being accepted. Maybe the news will be unexpected, but positive. This is also a good time to communicate with others without worrying whether your message will be received. It will come through loud and clear. You will also see this number when you've been beating yourself up over past actions. Are you lying awake at night going over things in your head? Do you have a hard time speaking kindly to yourself? You need to forgive yourself. When you do, a weight will be lifted. You'll feel freer and lighter. You may also have unexpected money headed your way when you see this number. This could take the form of a refund check you're not expecting, someone paying back a loan you never thought you'd see again, or winning a random raffle.

Affirmation: I will be kind to myself even when I make a mistake.

Activation: Write a letter to yourself to channel this angel number energy. We all have things we wish we hadn't done. Remember a moment in particular that you've had a hard time forgiving yourself for. Write that past you a letter of apology. Release yourself by realizing you're human, and that although the situation may have been painful, it served a purpose by being an experience from which you could grow.

Keywords: moving up, ease, new addition to the family

Meanings: You're moving up in life. This could be climbing the corporate ladder or reaching a level of status you've been striving for. Everything is falling into place, and you're being elevated. Your angels also like to send this number when you're moving into ease. If life has been a struggle, this is a welcome sight indeed. You'll notice love, money, and joy will find their way to you effortlessly. If you're thinking of starting a family, whether through pregnancy or adoption, seeing 123 is an excellent confirmation that soon your family will be expanding. If you're already expecting, this lets you know your pregnancy or adoption will go smoothly.

Affirmation: It's as easy at 1, 2, 3.

Activation: Since 123 is all about ease and moving up, try this to harness that feeling. For six days in a row, look in the mirror each morning and recite this chant: "As easy as 1, 2, 3, all I'm seeking will find me." When you make your intentions known, the Universe gets busy making them come true.

Keywords: surrendering, trusting in love, standing up for your beliefs

Meanings: Step aside for a while and let your angels pick up the slack. You've been carrying too much on your shoulders. Learn to surrender and offer up your problems to your angels. They love that stuff. Another message that may resonate with you is to trust in love. If you've had some heartaches, it's harder to open up to love because you're worried you'll get hurt again. But if you never try, you'll never know. If you're in a relationship that's going through a rocky patch, this message is sent as reassurance: If you follow your heart it won't guide you wrong. This number also shows up a lot when it's time for you to stick up for your beliefs. Perhaps you're heading home for the holidays, and your views are completely opposite from your parents' views. Don't be afraid to stand your ground. Even when it's difficult, you never know when something you say changes someone else's heart.

Affirmation: It's important to stand my ground.

Activation: Whenever you're in a situation where you feel unsure of yourself or know you'll be the odd person out, carry a piece of carnelian. This stone helps with self-esteem and fights any feelings of inadequacy or doubt. Carry it with you to strengthen your self-confidence.

Keywords: something's lacking, being held back, taking ownership

Meanings: Something is missing in your life. This is probably not a surprise to you, but your angels want you to do something about it. Life is too short to settle. Get proactive in your life and fix the problem. You'll also see this number when you're being held back. This could be coming from an inflexible significant other, a boss who undervalues you, or even yourself. Take time to sort out who's keeping you from your potential and take action to rectify it. Also, your angels will send this number when you need to take ownership of your part in your problems. Not everything is someone else's fault. More times than not, we simply don't want to own up to the fact that we got ourselves into a mess, and we need to get ourselves out.

Affirmation: I will no longer stand in my own way.

Activation: Sometimes, to take ownership of certain situations, it's good to reconnect with your Higher Self. The Higher Self is that part of the soul that remains in the spiritual realm while the rest of you comes down to incarnate on earth. This is the part of you that remembers everything you signed up for in this life cycle. To reconnect, light some dragon's blood incense. This helps clear anything clouding your aura. Then, lie down and place a piece of amethyst or clear quartz at the top of your head. Lie there for at least three minutes. Do this daily until you can sense that connection to your Higher Self again.

Keywords: commitment, persistence, take a trip

Meanings: Time to work on your commitment, whether to your career, your health, your relationship, or your personal growth. It can also mean your commitment has been above and beyond, and your angels commend your efforts. Your angels will also use this number to let you know they see your persistence, and they're proud of you. You could have given up a million times, but you didn't. That's to be applauded. Your angels will also encourage you to take a trip or vacation when you see this number. Take care of yourself so you don't burn out. Our culture may push work, work, work, but learning to relax and simply being is also important for your health and peace of mind.

Affirmation: Vacation time is me time.

Activation: This activation is simple. Go on a trip! Have a fabulous time.

Keywords: spiritual advancement, kindness, natural caregiver

Meanings: Your angels are acknowledging your spiritual advancement when they send this number. Maybe you've started a meditation practice and kept at it. Perhaps you finally started reading tarot or tea leaves for others. This is a part of your higher purpose, and your angels are pleased with your progress. Your angels will also send this number to commend you on your kindness to others. Typically, this shows up when you've gone above and beyond for others, but haven't received any gratitude or recognition for it. Not that you did it for the praise, but it feels hollow when you extend yourself for others and it goes unnoticed or unappreciated. Your angels appreciate what you've done. This number also appears when you're considering a job in health care or the service industry. You may already have a job in these areas, but they're in the field of traditional Western medicine. This message asks you to look at taking a turn into natural medicine because you have natural healing gifts and should use them.

Affirmation: From my overflowing cup, I pour into others.

Activation: To keep your cup full so you can help others, keep a glass of water on your bedside table near your head. The water will absorb any negative energy around you, keeping you feeling well and healthy so you can continue to help others. Empty the glass each morning, and refill it with fresh water each night.

Keywords: putting in the work, hobby to career, vulnerability

Meanings: Your angels are acknowledging how much work you've been doing. You could be either physically working hard, through work or exercise for your health, or putting in the work on yourself in other ways. All are praiseworthy, and that's the reason your angels send this message. If you've been considering creating a small business around a hobby, your angels are fully on board. Hobbies are an excellent way to release stress, but if you have a passion to make yours a full-time moneymaker, your angels are behind you. This number will also hound you when you need to be vulnerable. You might be the kind of person who takes care of everyone else and so feels like a burden when asking for help or showing vulnerability. Take down your walls. It takes a lot of strength to show your true self, and your angels are saying it's safe to do so.

Affirmation: My strength lies in my vulnerability.

Activation: Being vulnerable is difficult for many of us. If you'd like to work on it, try using a mirror to become more comfortable with yourself. Look in the mirror and make eye contact with yourself. Each day, tell yourself something loving. Point out one thing you like about yourself. Say, "I love you," or "We're safe now." This opens you not only to becoming more vulnerable with yourself, but also with others.

Keywords: try a different way, moving soon, dishonesty

Meanings: Loosen your approach, and try a different way to get to your goals. We're all guilty of getting stuck in a rut from time to time. This is your angels' way of asking you to think outside the box. Don't be too rigid in your approach to life. Sometimes, you have to try something new to keep it fresh. You will also see this angel number when you're moving soon. Maybe you want a job in a new city or you're simply bored with your current location. This is your angels confirming that a move at this time is ideal. This message can also show up when someone you're dealing with is being dishonest. Your angels don't like to bring you bad news, but if negative information will help you resolve an issue, they'll do it. Keep your antennae up to spot the untrustworthy person in your circle.

Affirmation: I'm flexible and willing to try a different approach.

Activation: Try this to figure out when someone is being dishonest. Use a blue candle to represent the person you want the truth from. Carve their name into the candle. Light the candle. As it burns, state your intentions. Explain that as the candle burns, they'll feel an intense burning inside to speak the truth. Make sure the candle burns all the way out (never leave burning candles unattended). Once completely cool, dispose of the candle in the trash. Sit back and wait for truths to be revealed.

Keywords: perfect timing, stay present, positive karma

Meanings: Right now, the timing is perfect for whatever you want to do with your life. Thinking of a new job? Do it. Want to move? Go for it. Considering a new romance? Fire up those dating apps. You may also see this angel number if you're drifting a little too far into the past or forward into the future. This is a gentle reminder to remember that the present is a gift and to keep your attention here. Use a grounding technique to keep you in the here and now. Your angels will also use this number when you're due for some positive karma. You may already be experiencing it or soon will be. It's not a coincidence but, rather, a matter of hard work and good deeds on your part.

Affirmation: Everything works out in its perfect time.

Activation: If you find yourself chasing daydreams or reliving past moments, carry a piece of smoky quartz with you. It grounds you and keeps you in the present moment.

Keywords: learning experience, fulfilling romance, claircognizance

Meanings: Your angels send this number when things are a little rocky. You may be questioning why things have happened the way they have or what the point of it all is. You need to see it as a learning experience. You're going to be able to apply this information to future problems. If you're on the lookout for a romantic partner or want a deeper connection in your current relationship, this is a timely message to receive. You're about to move into a very fulfilling romantic relationship. Another time you'll see this number is when you suddenly start having deep insights or simply knowing something without any other information. This is known as claircognizance, or clear knowing. Your angels are encouraging you to study up on it and confirming that, yes, you do have this ability.

Affirmation: I deserve a deep and fulfilling love.

Activation: To strengthen claircognizance, follow your instincts. When you receive a truly psychic insight, it will be disconnected from any emotional response. That's how you can differentiate between your thoughts or anxiety and those that predict the future. When you get an intuitive hit, feel into it. How do you feel? Anxious? Nervous? Or suspiciously without emotion in that moment? Take note of what happens when you follow these insights. The more you work on it, the stronger your ability will become.

Keywords: empowerment, overcoming anxiety, spiritual high five

Meanings: Either you're currently feeling empowered, or you should feel empowered soon, to take whatever steps you need to make your life the way you want it. You are a limitless soul having a human experience. You can accomplish whatever you set your intentions on. Be empowered to be the hero of your story. This number is also used when you're dealing with anxiety. If you're someone who struggles daily with this issue, know that you have the ability to overcome it, and your angels will help you with it. This number also shows up when your angels send you a spiritual high five. It's like a slap on the back or an attaboy from the spiritual realm for a recent spiritual success, such as not sinking to someone else's level or acting as your authentic self.

Affirmation: By taking small steps, my anxiety can become manageable.

Activation: To feel more empowered in your daily life, sleep with a tiger's eye stone under your bed. You can also carry it in your purse, wallet, or pocket. This stone boosts confidence and courage and will have you feeling ready for whatever is thrown your way.

Keywords: job opportunity, problem solved, inner child healing

Meanings: A job opportunity is on its way to you. This is rewarding to hear if you've been in the job market for a while. This can also represent getting a promotion or moving up in your current position. If you've been worried about a problem you can't seem to solve, your angels want you to know that the problem is being resolved for you. This message comes to give you peace and comfort. Know that it will be okay. This angel number also shows up when you're going through some inner child healing. You may have started therapy to work on this, or you may need to if you're experiencing nightmares from that period of your life. If you're having a difficult time with it, know that your angels are there to support you through the entire journey.

Affirmation: I am now the safe space my inner child always needed.

Activation: Do this inner child meditation if you'd like to offer healing to yourself, past and present. Sit in a quiet area where you won't be disturbed. Close your eyes and take several deep breaths. In your mind's eye, imagine yourself at the age you may have suffered some trauma or pain as a child. Ask this younger version of yourself what you needed at that time. Listen, and without judgment, accept what answers come up. Explain to that child that although the past can't be changed, in the present you're safe and loved. Give that child a hug. Stay in this space as long as you're comfortable. Tears will most likely flow. Let them fall. This is deeply healing and restorative to your soul.

Keywords: good fortune, relaxation, better family relationships

Meanings: Your luck is looking up. Good fortune is coming your way. This can range from an extra $20 found in your pocket to receiving a massive raise. Relish having a turn of fortune in which you have the upper hand. Your angels will also send this number to ask you to relax. You can't rush around at all times. This is a gentle nudge to recharge your batteries. Eat a snack, take a relaxing bath, or book a trip to Cabo. Do nothing productive at all. Make time simply to relax. Also, if you see this number again and again, you can look forward to better family relationships. Maybe there's been some division or a rift in your family. Perhaps you've had a hard time communicating with your teenagers or partner. Your angels always want you to have peace and harmony, and so, when the timing is right, they'll send this message of hope and reconciliation to bolster your spirits.

Affirmation: I encourage good fortune to find me always.

Activation: To attract more wealth to your door, try this feng shui cure. Purchase a fortune frog—a golden statue of a three-legged frog that sits on a pile of coins with a coin in its mouth. It is said to bring prosperity when you place it facing your front door.

Keywords: clairaudience, unconditional love, new pet coming in

Meanings: You most likely have clear hearing, also known as clairaudience. You may have started hearing things you can't explain. Maybe as you're drifting off to sleep, someone calls your name. Your angels want to assure you that you're not losing it. This is a real skill emerging and the angels are encouraging you to work with it. You also see this angel number when unconditional love is needed in your life, either from yourself or from someone else. You deserve love that comes with no strings attached, and when you see this number, it's on its way to you. Also, you may have a special animal soul coming into your life soon. You might find a stray you bring home and love. Perhaps you're contemplating a pet adoption. Your angels send this as a confirmation to bring that fur baby home right away.

Affirmation: I deserve to be loved just as I am.

Activation: If you're interested in strengthening your clairaudience, try this. Pay attention to everything you listen to. When listening to music, isolate different instruments. Try to pick out different voices and tones. Also, pay attention to your mind's internal chatter. Do you find songs play randomly in your head? Do you hear snippets of conversation that don't belong to you? Tuning in hones your ability to differentiate between random sounds and communication from Spirit. With time and dedication, this skill can be used to relay messages to others from their angels, guides, and loved ones in spirit. Keep listening—you'll be surprised at what will come through.

Keywords: patience, acceptance, laughter

Meanings: You may be in a hurry for a specific manifestation to appear or goal to be achieved, but your angels are advising you gently to sit tight. Things will work out in their own time. Demonstrate some patience while they do. Acceptance is another message your angels send with this number. You may need to work on accepting some parts of your life or yourself. Perhaps you're already working on that. Your angels praise you for taking this step. You will also see this angel number when you need more laughter. Such a simple concept, but laughter is very important to life. Taking yourself or life too seriously is a recipe for disaster. Turn on your favorite comedy or spend time with that friend who always makes you laugh. It not only alleviates stress, but raises your overall frequency.

Affirmation: I'm working on accepting all facets of my life.

Activation: If you want to harness more laughter in your life in a powerful way, try laughing yoga. This practice combines breathing techniques with laughter, which will result in increased energy levels. Studies have shown that cortisol levels can be reduced by this exercise, and your outlook will be positively affected.

Meanings: It's time to remove the toxicity from your life. This harmful energy may involve a work situation, relationship, or even media you watch. Your angels are helping you remove that negativity. Once gone from your life, you will feel a lift in your energy levels. Also, you will see this number to alert you to the fact that your clairsentience is strengthening. Clairsentience, also known as clear feeling, is a psychic sense that allows you to gain information through your feelings. You may be picking up on other people's emotions, experiencing them so deeply that they feel like your own. Maybe when you touch an object, you get flashes of insight from it. You have a natural gift and should utilize it. Your angels are as concerned about your physical health as they are your spiritual life. Perhaps you've been caught up in the hubbub of life, but now's the time to schedule that doctor visit you've been putting off or see your therapist to check in on your mental health.

Affirmation: I will make my health a priority.

Activation: You will need a partner for this exercise. Sit facing someone and hold hands. Both people should close their eyes. Advise your partner to think of an emotional memory. Once they tell you they have it in mind, notice how your body feels. Did your body temperature change? Tingling? Are there any emotions floating to the surface? Crying? Laughing? Feel all the feels. Then, let your partner relay the memory and advise how much information you received correctly. The more you practice this, the better you'll get.

Keywords: set boundaries, tie up loose ends, believe in your magic

Meanings: You need to set some healthy boundaries. Your angels see every facet of your life, and their job is to guide, nudge, and advise you. That's their aim when they send this angel number. People are taking advantage of your kindhearted nature and need to be reminded to respect your time, space, and energy. There are many books and videos on this subject. You can always seek professional help as well. You will also receive this angel number when you need to tie up loose ends. You may be close to finishing a project or goal, but you're not taking care of a few small things. Now's the moment. If there's still some of your stuff at an ex's, let's go pick that up. It's hard to move forward with loose strings around to snag you. Your angels also really love to see you shine, but sometimes life dulls your light. Perhaps your confidence has waned, or you're struggling with a certain situation. Your angels will help you get back into the groove so you can believe in your magic again. The world needs your shine.

Affirmation: Setting boundaries creates healthy relationships.

Activation: When you attempt to set boundaries, some people will push back. If you want to have your home feel like a sanctuary and safe space, place tourmaline crystals at each door of your home. This powerful crystal helps protect you and creates an invisible boundary around your home. You'll be surprised how those with ill intentions react when attempting to cross your threshold once these crystals are in place.

Keywords: taking your power back, stress easing,
hearing from an old friend

Meanings: Your angels are there to help in every situation life throws your way. One of those is feeling disempowered. It happens to all of us. Bad moments happen, and narratives are formed. Work to acknowledge what happened. Facing it will help you move on and reconnect you to your power. You'll also see this number when you're completely frazzled. It normally shows up right on time when you're about to pull out your hair over tense situations. Before you do, take a deep breath and know that those stressors will be easing. You may also be hearing from an old friend when you see angel number 54. A phone call or text out of the blue is possible as well as visitations that cross time and space, such as dreaming of a friend who has passed. Even though it's a dream, don't discount it because, many times, those in spirit will visit us this way. Listen carefully to your loved one's words. They could hold a powerful message.

Affirmation: I'm moving into an era of minimal stress.

Activation: If you want help taking your power back in situations where you feel there's an imbalance, here's a simple fix. In tarot, the high priestess represents someone who truly owns her power. Carry this card with you when having difficult conversations or facing situations where you could use a little extra empowerment.

Keywords: new journey, ancestor pride, family reconciliation

Meanings: You're about to start a new journey, which can include career, health, or even spiritual journeys. Your angels are with you. Also, your ancestors use this angel number to let you know how proud they are of you. It's not so much your accomplishments (those are nice), but it's more about the person you've become. You are an excellent representative for your family. When there is a chance for reconciliation, specifically within your family, you will also see this angel number. Perhaps there has been discord, and you've been distanced. There is an opening for healing. You may be surprised when your family members are receptive to working on the relationship.

Affirmation: A new journey awaits.

Activation: Honor your ancestors. You can make this as simple or as complex as you'd like. Those who came before us set the path we now travel. Hang ancestors' pictures in your home. Cook their recipes. Light a candle in remembrance. You can even have an altar on which to place their favorite foods and items.

Keywords: gaining freedom, stability, good deeds acknowledged

Meanings: You'll soon gain your freedom. This doesn't necessarily mean being freed from a physical prison, although it could. However, in most instances, it refers to gaining freedom from a situation in which you've felt trapped. A door has opened that will take you to a new job, relationship, or situation. Your angels will also let you know that stability will return to your situation. This message confirms that brighter days are ahead, and the path forward is being cleared for you. Your angels may also be acknowledging the good deeds you've done for others when you see this number. Those good deeds feed your karma and have not gone unnoticed.

Affirmation: I am no longer trapped by my situation.

Activation: Many times, when you feel stuck or imprisoned by a situation, it's almost like someone else is pulling the strings. So, it's time to cut yourself loose! Find an object to represent yourself. It can be a water bottle, a brush, really any object around that size. Then, take some string and wrap it around the object. Once you've finished, grab a pair of scissors. Before cutting, say, "I now free myself from _____ (whatever you'd like freedom from). As I cut these strings, my situation is improving, and my freedom is coming." Then, cut each string until they all fall away. Gather up the object that represents you and the cut strings and place them in a brown paper bag. Dispose of the bag at either 7:00 a.m. or 6:00 p.m.

Keywords: childhood sweethearts, volunteering, need for solitude

Meanings: Did you have a sweetheart you lost touch with or simply grew apart from after graduating school? Are you single or in a transitional state in your life? When you see this angel number, a special romance may be rekindled. Another time you'll see this angel number is when you begin to help others through volunteering. A major part of everyone's purpose on earth is to help each other. Your angels like to pat you on the back when they see you're fulfilling that mission. You may also see this number when you need some alone time. The world can get noisy with all its deadlines and responsibilities. When this message resonates, carve out some time for solitude, even if only a few hours.

Affirmation: By extending a hand to others, I impact the world in a positive way.

Activation: Find peace in your own bubble of solitude. Sometimes, it's just not possible to find time alone, especially if you live with other people. So, try this when you can't be alone. Sit wherever you are and close your eyes. Take three slow, deep breaths. Imagine a bubble in front of you. Slowly it grows bigger and bigger until it's large enough to fit over your entire body. Watch as it floats over you and encloses you fully. Once you're inside the bubble, feel how your body changes. Relax your shoulders and calves. Release the tension in your jaw. Set the intention that while inside this bubble you're alone, safe, and at peace.

Keywords: reach out, reconnect with spirituality,
don't settle for less

Meanings: Your angels will send this message to those warrior spirits like you who are always looking out for others, but rarely reach out for help themselves. They are asking you to reach out to friends, family, or a professional to get some help. Take care of you so you can continue to take care of others. Your angels will also send this message when you need to reconnect with your spiritual roots. Your angels don't care which spiritual path you follow. They simply want you to address the issue at hand, which, most likely, will need some spiritual practice to fix. Your angels will also send this number when you've been undervaluing yourself. Don't settle for less than your worth. That might mean taking another job or leaving a relationship that doesn't treat you fairly.

Affirmation: I know my worth, and I won't settle for less.

Activation: Boost your self-worth and empower yourself by carrying a piece of citrine. This crystal is called the sunshine stone because of its hue and its ability to bring light into any area of your life. This is an especially effective crystal when asking for a raise or more from a relationship.

Keywords: cut back, don't be afraid, spirit visitations

Meanings: You need to cut back on excesses. If you're overworking, cut back on the amount of time spent at the office. If you're indulging in some bad habits, reassess your priorities. This is a gentle nudge from your angels to get you back on track. You will also receive this number when you're scared. Your angels are reassuring you that there's no reason to be afraid. Perhaps you're dealing with a situation that taps into a deep-seated fear and you're not sure if you can handle it. Your angels know you can. Stop worrying about all the what-ifs. You are so much braver than you give yourself credit for. Your angels also like to send this message because you've been receiving spirit visitations. Have weird things been going on around your house? Do you think you've seen something out of the corner of your eye? Are your dreams strange? This is a confirmation that you are, in fact, dealing with spirits.

Affirmation: It's time to reprioritize my life.

Activation: Spirit visitations, no matter how loving or well-meaning, can be unsettling. If you're finding the spirit activity in your home reaching an uncomfortable level, do this to reclaim your space. Make a statement aloud that, within your home, only those entities of pure love and light are allowed. All other entities must go. No negativity is allowed to dwell in your space. You can do this in each room while using a cleansing element such as Florida water, holy water, or incense.

Keywords: honesty, stressed out, breakthrough

Meanings: Are you being 100 percent honest with yourself? Do you worry that someone close to you is lying? Whatever situation you're facing requires honesty, and that's why your angels are sending you this number. It's hard to face the truth sometimes, but when you do, you will feel lighter afterward. You may also see this number when you're stressed out. Perhaps you've been pushed to your breaking point. Your angels hate to see you distressed. They see your concerns, and they're sending help. You can also receive this angel number when a major breakthrough is on the way. This is a great message to receive when life feels stagnant—yours is about to change in a major way.

Affirmation: My breakthrough is coming.

Activation: In order to de-stress, align with the angel number 432 by listening to sounds that resonate at 432 Hz. It helps with stress, soothing and calming you. It also helps release emotional blockages. Beyond that, use those tried-and-true methods specific to you that help lower your stress level.

DECIPHERING ANGEL NUMBERS

Keywords: clouds are lifting, stay open-minded, Christ energy

Meanings: Have you been blue? Does the atmosphere in your life seem heavy? Your angels send this message to tell you that the clouds are lifting. They're aware of what you're going through, and they're sending you a ray of sunshine. Your angels will also nudge you gently when you need to be a little more open-minded. Maybe you're in a tiff with someone, and you refuse to see their side of the argument. Maybe it's time to give up some long-held beliefs that are not only outdated but also harmful if you hold on to them. This angel number also resonates with Christ energy. You may need to apply a little of Christ's example to your own life. It can also indicate that this energy is entering your life for you to work with ritualistically and spiritually.

Affirmation: With an open mind, I grow and learn more every day.

Activation: To welcome Christ energy into your life, whether you consider yourself a Christian or not, do this. Place a picture or statue of Christ on your altar. Ask for His intercession on your behalf with issues you're having. Also, channeling Christ energy can help center and guide you.

Keywords: lack of confidence, reflect on your purpose, letting go

Meanings: When you're struggling with confidence, your angels send this number. They want you to know you have no reason to doubt yourself or your abilities. Whatever you want to pursue, give it your all. They're cheering you on. This angel number also comes up when you've been thinking about your purpose. Your angels want to help you meet that purpose. So, call on them for help. This may also be a time when you need to learn to let go. You may be hanging on to someone or something that needs to be released. This also relates to letting go of the need to control outcomes. Release it to the Universe and be pleasantly surprised.

Affirmation: I release the need to control.

Activation: Journal to help figure out your purpose. You can have many purposes in one lifetime. Use these prompts to help you focus on your purpose(s).

- What lights me up? What is it that I can't imagine life without? Music? Art? Words? Animals? That's a great place to start.
- What do I dream/daydream about, and what catches my attention when I hear about it? This could be telling toward my purpose.
- If I were to pursue some of these paths, what unique quality do I bring to them? What do I think I can bring to this area?

Keywords: Buddha energy, animal spirits, next level love

Meanings: Buddha energy is moving into your life. You may be studying Buddhism or questioning it. This is your angel's acknowledgment that you're on the right track. Your angels will also use this number to make you aware that animal spirits are visiting you. Have you had a precious fur baby pass over? Have you felt like you've heard animals or sensed them? If you're seeing this number a lot, then you certainly have. They will visit you in low moments or anytime you need an extra love boost. This angel number is also sent when your romantic life is about to move to the next level. You may finally start to receive the commitment you've craved or the connection is deepening in an entirely new way.

Affirmation: The love in my life is expanding and moving to new levels.

Activation: Buddha energy is all about mindfulness. You can harness this energy through meditation, but also bring it in through a Buddha statue or image placed on your sacred space. Ask to channel Buddha's energy when you sleep, and note the difference you experience upon waking.

Keywords: truths revealed, slow down, let it be

Meanings: There are things you've known for a long time, but it seems those around you are falling for others' lies. Don't sweat it because truths are about to revealed. You won't have to lift a finger for the curtain to fall, and reality will be exposed. Your angels also want what's best for you. So, if you're busy scurrying about from task to task, they will ask you to slow down. This could be a mild warning as it may affect your health—mental or physical. Also, your angels will send this number when you need to let it be. You might be trying to fix a problem that's out of your control or worrying over something you can't change. They bring this as comfort. The Universe is in control. Let it be, and be at peace.

Affirmation: Life is not a race. I will take my time.

Activation: Try this to help soothe your soul and lessen your worries. This takes three days and invokes the energy of 876. On the first day at 8:00 p.m., write down what you want to let the Universe work out. Place the piece of paper on a table and take three steps back while facing it, then turn away. On the second night at 7:00 p.m., while standing before the paper you wrote last night, think about what you wrote. Then, take two steps back, and turn away. On the third night at 6:00 p.m., speak aloud what you wrote down, take one step back, then turn away. Thank your angels for their help. Then, throw away the paper and, as you do, your worries about this situation go with it.

Keywords: Mother Mary energy, take responsibility, don't hide your emotions

Meanings: Mother Mary, Jesus's mother, will be entering your life in a spiritual way. You may find yourself interested in her story. You may start to feel a peaceful energy helping you on your path. You don't have to consider yourself a Christian to work with her energy. Your angels will also send this number to guide you gently to take responsibility for a situation. Perhaps you're being a bit stubborn in admitting fault, or you're procrastinating on a situation that needs to be resolved. Take a look at yourself to see if there are steps you can take to help. You will also see this angel number if you're someone who carries your cards close to your chest. Your angels are nudging you to open up a bit more. Don't hide your emotions. If something has upset you, but you've kept it to yourself, let it out. Respect your emotions and give them an outlet.

Affirmation: I own my part in this situation and take full responsibility.

Activation: Mother Mary is a great source of strength and represents a conduit between this world and the next. So, she can be used as a representation of bringing things forth from the spiritual plane. You can add her to your altar through an image or statue. You can also ask for her help with issues surrounding motherhood, inner strength, and patience.

Keywords: change of heart, at goal, nothing else required

Meanings: Either you or someone close to you is soon to have a change of heart. Maybe you're beginning to see a situation in a different light. Perhaps someone opens up and offers an apology you never saw coming. This is all possible at this time. Also, your angels love to send this number when you're very close to reaching a goal. As the countdown of the number itself indicates, you're close to reaching zero, when everything's done. That finish line is close. Your angels will also send this number to let you know nothing else is required. You don't have to wait to start a project or take another class before heading out on your own. It's good to be prepared, but don't get stuck in analysis paralysis.

Affirmation: I have everything I need to begin.

Activation: Use the magician card from a tarot deck to help you channel the angel number 4321. In tarot, the magician represents having all the tools you need to accomplish your goals. You don't need to wait or gather any more information before starting. Carry this card with you to get started on whatever you've been hesitating about.

Keywords: increasing intuition, walk your own path, building wealth

Meanings: You're about to have an increase in intuition. You may notice knowing things without knowing how. You may find your instincts are really strong. You could also have flashes of insight that lead to really good outcomes. Your angels will also use this number to confirm you're right to walk your own path. You can't be someone else, even if you try. You shouldn't have to. Your angels applaud you for living your life on your terms. This is also a great angel number to see with regard to finances. You're entering a phase of life in which you can build wealth that will serve you for years to come.

Affirmation: Whether it's understood or not, I choose to walk my own way.

Activation: Our bodies have seven major energy centers, also known as chakras. When you want to increase intuition, work with your crown chakra. It is the gateway between this world and the next. It sits at the top of your head, hence the term "crown." You can meditate with a clear quartz or amethyst on top of your head, either sitting or lying down. Proceed to do a golden light meditation in which you imagine a golden, shimmering light entering through your crown chakra to open it up. Sit in this light for at least five minutes. Do this whenever you want to open your crown chakra or receive stronger intuitive hits.

Keywords: loyalty, overcoming challenges, ease your mind

Meanings: You are a loyal person. You are always there to support those closest to you, and that means something. Perhaps you're questioning whether someone is being loyal to you. Let this be a confirmation that, if you're unsure about this person, you probably have good reason. Your angels will also send this number when you're about to overcome challenges. You may have been struggling for a while now and, possibly, are ready to give up. Hang in there. You're going to make it through. Also, your angels want to ease your mind because stressors will be decreasing. Take some mental health days to rebalance and refresh.

Affirmation: Even though this is challenging, I can make it through.

Activation: A challenge can sometimes seem insurmountable. What if you could take your problem and chop it down to size? Well, you can. Take a piece of paper and draw a large mountain on it. Make sure it fills the entire page. Label the mountain with the issue you're facing. For the next nine days, cut away a small piece of the paper from the bottom up. On the ninth and final day, cut the last piece, leaving you with a much more manageable mountain. This symbology prepares your mind to see your current issue as a much more manageable one to tackle.

Keywords: higher calling, gifted, feeling restless

Meanings: You have a special calling in life. You may be destined to work in a spiritual leader capacity, such as a pastor, priestess, or shaman. Maybe this is something you're already thinking about, and seeing this message gives you confirmation of pursuing that calling. Your angels also send this message when you're gifted with special talents. You may be aware that you possess special skills, but you're not ready to admit it fully. Now is the time to accept these gifts and, ultimately, use them. This angel number also appears when you've been feeling a little on edge. Work or a relationship may be lacking. Instead of ignoring it away, your angels always suggest addressing and resolving the problem. That restlessness occurs for a reason. Honor yourself by getting to the bottom of it.

Affirmation: I honor the restlessness in my body and know it's time for change.

Activation: Do an energy scan of your body. Sitting upright, use your right hand as a wand. Beginning at the top of your head, slowly glide your hand down your body. As you do so, take stock of how your body feels. Did your heart rate change? Did you get a tingle? Did your temperature go suddenly cold or hot? Pay attention to those feelings, as they're telling you where you have restlessness. Once you know where that energy resides in your body, send cleansing white light to it. Imagine a brilliant shower of light flooding that area. Journal afterward to document how you felt before, during, and after the body scan.

8765

Keywords: comfort, step away, ancestral inheritance

Meanings: Your angels are sending you comfort. They know you're going through an emotionally difficult time, and they want you to feel better. You may find that when crying or lying in bed, you feel a gentle calming presence. Don't worry. It's only your angels. If you find yourself in a situation where someone is making you feel uncomfortable or your boundaries are overstepped, your angels will send this number to advise you to step away from the situation. Giving yourself some space is a healthy way to deal with this. Don't be afraid to limit certain people's access to you if they continually show they don't respect you. You'll also see this number when you've been chosen to continue an ancestral tradition. Maybe you're an excellent cook like your grandmother or extremely creative like your great-aunt. This talent is no coincidence, but has been passed down to you from your ancestors. If this resonates with you, express gratitude to your ancestors and thank them for the gifts.

Affirmation: I will remove myself from situations that infringe on my boundaries.

Activation: Everyone needs comforting from time to time. When you can't find someone to be with you during a difficult time, engage in some self-soothing. Treat yourself with a favorite movie, food, exercise, hobby, etc. Don't place any judgment on what you find comforting. When you're in a vulnerable spot, you deserve extra self-care.

Keywords: don't lose hope, socialize, take the reins

Meanings: Lift your head up. You may feel at the end of your rope, but don't despair. Brighter days are ahead. Your angels see your situation, and they're sending you strength to help you through this difficult time. Also, your angels see you at all times and, when they sense you need a nudge in a certain direction, they'll send one. Have you become withdrawn? Are you as social as you used to be? We all tend to close ourselves off after something stressful occurs. But we're all interconnected in this life. Recharge your batteries by spending time with friends and loved ones. Hit your favorite restaurant or hot spot to remember there's life beyond your front door. It's time for you to take charge of your life when you see this angel number. If there's a situation in which you're taking a back seat to someone that you shouldn't be, that needs to end. Take the reins and be assertive. You have a legion of angels at your back to help you stand up for yourself.

Affirmation: It's time to get out and about.

Activation: Many people don't socialize as much because it drains their energy. To help keep your social battery charged during social interactions, carry black onyx. This keeps you more energetic and receptive during otherwise draining encounters.

PATTERNED NUMBERS

Numbers that follow a certain sequence, such as 135, where a particular pattern is seen, are known as patterned numbers. They are arranged in a way that follows a specific order or rule. Because of their uniqueness, these numbers represent another effective way for your angels to get your attention and send you messages. This section could go on and on as numbers in all their different combinations are limitless. However, the following numbers are the most frequently used patterned angel numbers.

Keywords: clear your energetic space, get organized, open to channeling

Meanings: It's time to clear your energetic space. With each interaction we have with another human or the environment, we encounter energy. It's like static electricity that can build up in your socks as you walk. So, there are times when you need to release that accumulated energy. You can try several techniques, such as smoke, holy water, or crystal cleansing. This is also a push from your angels to get organized. This could be something practical like organizing paperwork or cleaning your home, or refer to organizing your thoughts, making sure to set down goals and begin working on them. You can also receive this number when you're open to channeling. Channeling is a spiritual gift that allows you to enter a meditative state and receive information from the spiritual realm. You may or may not be aware of this ability, but if you're interested in pursuing it, this is your sign to take up its study as you have an innate gift.

Affirmation: When I sort my surroundings, I feel more prepared for the day.

Activation: If cleaning and organizing isn't your thing, start with one hour at a time. Set a timer, put on your favorite tunes, and work diligently for one hour. Once the timer goes off, take a break. Acknowledge how much you accomplished in such a short period of time. Little by little, you can take care of whatever tasks lay before you.

Keywords: closing a chapter, receiving recognition, thinking it through

Meanings: One chapter is closing so a new phase can begin. A new job may open up, whereas another will be left behind. One relationship could end, only to open new pathways for love. Although endings can be sad, the one you're facing will lead to better outcomes. You will also see this angel number when you're going to receive recognition. This can range from a major award to a simple recognition by a friend or family member for something you've done for them. Either way, in whatever form it comes, you deserve it. This angel number also appears when you're dealing with a situation that requires contemplation. Your angels are supporting you while you think things through and are impressed with how thoroughly you're working through this.

Affirmation: As one chapter closes, I know a new adventure awaits.

Activation: To encapsulate the ending of one chapter fully in order to herald the beginning of a new one, try this exercise. At 1:00 p.m., walk through a doorway in your home. As you do, say, "As one door closes, another opens" one time. The next time you walk through that doorway, say it again three times. The next and last time you walk through this door, say it again, increasing it to five times. This not only primes your subconscious for the changes coming, but also sends the intention to the Universe that you're ready.

Keywords: self-reliant, seeker, problem solver

Meanings: Your angels are acknowledging your self-reliance. They know you haven't always had someone to lean on, but that didn't stop you. You have this inner strength to get the job done no matter what. Don't forget to ask for help when you do need it, though. Your angels will provide it. You also have a seeker's heart when you see this angel number. Your angels are with you on the journey and will help you find answers. They are urging you to keep seeking. If you're a problem solver, this angel number will find you. You like to figure out a solution when others can't. You find a way. Your angels admire this quality. Keep tackling those problems!

Affirmation: I'm a seeker of truth, wisdom, and myself.

Activation: If you face a situation that needs a solution, sometimes putting it on ice can help. Literally. If something is troubling you, an irksome coworker perhaps, try this simple technique. Write their name on a piece of paper and place it inside a freezer bag. Fill the bag with water, then stick it in the freezer. See if the situation with this person doesn't cool down, giving you time to sort out the problem.

Keywords: empath, swept off your feet, saving

Meanings: You are a true empath. That word gets thrown around a lot these days, but your sensitivity is real. You have the ability to feel what others truly feel. Learn how to protect yourself with shields so that tapping into others' energy doesn't drain you. This angel number may also appear as you're about to be swept off your feet in a head-first romance. This has all the butterflies and tingles. If you're hesitating at all to date this person, don't. It's the real thing. Your angels will also send this number to bring your finances to the forefront. Maybe you're overspending, or they know of an upcoming issue that will require extra cash. If you receive this message, start saving money. It doesn't have to be a huge amount. Every little bit helps.

Affirmation: My strength lies in my sensitivity to others.

Activation: As an empath, you will need to learn how to shield yourself so you don't become drained by interactions with others. Before leaving your house, imagine a force field encircling your entire body. Set the intention that, while you're out and about, this shield will keep others' emotions from affecting you. Once you've done this visualization a few times, you can simply say, "Shield up" or "Protection on" and you'll be safe around others.

Keywords: rejoice, believe in yourself, say no

Meanings: You have reason to rejoice when you receive this angel number. Your angels are joining you in celebration. Get ready for joy because something you've been wishing for is coming to pass! Now is the time to believe in yourself when you see this angel number. Your angels are encouraging you to take the steps needed to begin a new project by first believing you can. Don't let doubts stop you. If you're a people-pleaser or can't seem to find the word "no," your angels are urging you to figure it out. Although it may be hard to say at first, the more you practice, the better you get at it, not to mention the better you feel after doing it.

Affirmation: The first step to setting healthy boundaries is learning to say "no."

Activation: Saying "no" may be new to you, and so, at first it will be difficult. Since the angel number 212 reduces down to the number 5, here are five ways to say "no" without actually saying "no" until you get more comfortable with it. Try these:

- Not this time.
- I'm afraid I can't.
- Thanks, but I can't make it.
- My plate's full at the moment.
- I have another commitment.

Keywords: resolving old trauma, making progress, soul searching

Meanings: You're resolving old trauma with the help of your angels. You may have taken steps such as therapy or healing modalities. Your angels want to congratulate you on your effort. There's also progress being made if you see this angel number. Perhaps you're on a journey to improve your health or going back to school to move up in your career. Your angels see the progress you're making, and they're rooting you on. And if you feel like you haven't made any progress, take real stock of what you've done so far. Your angels don't bring it up for no reason. You may also see this angel number if you've been doing some soul searching lately. Perhaps you're trying to figure out your next move. Maybe you feel rudderless and without guidance. Your angels are letting you know that they see you and are helping you find clarity on your path.

Affirmation: Every step taken counts as progress made.

Activation: To symbolize the progress you're making, or potentially want to make, take a week to try this. Each day, speak aloud at least one step you're taking toward progress. For example, it can be as simple as, "I made sure to shower, dress, and show up fully for the day." When you begin acknowledging your progress, it becomes that much easier to see it.

Keywords: manifesting magic, change in fortune, satisfying result

Meanings: It's a great time to manifest your desires when you see this angel number. It's one of those rare moments in life when everything simply flows as you want it to. Take advantage of the momentum. This is why your angels sent this message your way. You can also see a change in fortune when you find this angel number. If you've been down on your luck, this is great news. However, it can also be a warning that your fortunes may be changing soon. So, be prepared. Also, when you see this angel number, you're going to end up with a satisfying result on whatever current project you're working on. Maybe you're about to run out of steam, or question whether it's even worth it. Keep plugging away because your angels know you'll like the results.

Affirmation: I believe in my potential to create my reality.

Activation: Utilize the 2-4-6 method to help your manifestations happen more quickly. Decide what you'd like to manifest. Then, write down your intentions twice in the morning. At midday, write down those same intentions four times. Before bed, write down your intentions six more times. Start this on a new moon and journal in this manner for the next thirty days. Make sure to write what you want in the present tense as if you already have it. For example, "I'm so thankful for the extra $50,000 in my bank account." Give it a month and see what magic occurs.

Keywords: finances improving, changing social circle, rebirth

Meanings: Your money situation is improving. If cash has been tight or bills seem too many, thank your angels when you see this number. Things are turning in your favor. Also, your angels want you to know that everyone can't go with you. What does that mean? Well, when you move into new levels of growth, some people don't resonate with that new frequency. You're in an outgrowing phase, as in old situations and people. You may also be about to experience a rebirth of sorts when you're sent this angel number. Perhaps you've gone through a health scare recently that's put you on a healing path. You feel like an entirely new person. Enjoy this time. You're like a butterfly emerging from its cocoon. Get ready to fly.

Affirmation: Life happens in cycles, and I'm ready for a rebirth.

Activation: To symbolize your rebirth, use a butterfly as a lucky charm. You can wear clothing with butterflies on it, accessorize with them, find jewelry with butterflies, place a picture of a butterfly on your altar, or any other manner you see fit. This channels that energy even stronger as you emerge from your rebirthing phase.

Keywords: curiosity, renewal, conquering fears

Meanings: You're an inquisitive, curious person. Curiosity is a good thing. Your angels send this number to encourage you to be more inquisitive. Maybe there are areas of your life in which you're not asking enough questions. Don't hold back. Be nosy about what's happening in *your* life. Also, when you see this angel number, there is a sense of renewal. Maybe your spirits are low because of the trials and tribulations you've faced. Your angels want you to know that your situation is being renewed. There is fresh energy coming. Also, if you've been attempting to overcome a fear, your angels see your efforts and praise you. Your angels know you will conquer those fears. You were intended to live your life to its fullest, and that's just what you will do.

Affirmation: I will not be held back by my fears.

Activation: Do you fear spiders? Maybe snakes? Or heights? Maybe it's more along the lines of not making your dreams come true. Let's take those fears and make them less scary. Find something that represents one of your fears. For example, if you're scared of big dogs, find a stuffed toy puppy. Talk to it each day. Make friends with it. Start to see your fear as something that's not very scary at all. When you can do that, you're that much closer to overcoming the fear.

Keywords: unique, take a chance, begin meditation

Meanings: You are a unique soul. Your angels want you to lean into that individuality because that's where your purpose lies. You're not here to be like everyone else. Be your exceptional self! You will also see this angel number when it's time to take chances. Be a little more risky. Push yourself outside of your comfort zone. Your angels wouldn't send you this encouragement if they weren't going to help you. You may also see this angel number when you need to start meditating. This practice is not only for those who want to attain spiritual skills. You can introduce meditation into your life as a way to center yourself and alleviate stress.

Affirmation: I'm going to take a chance on myself.

Activation: Use the 3-4-3 technique to begin your meditation journey. Take three deep breaths, counting to four on each inhalation, then exhale. Once you feel centered, sit quietly with your thoughts for three minutes. That's all you need to get started. Do this until you're ready to sit longer. Meditation doesn't have to be long to be effective.

Keywords: tap into potential, collaborate, childhood memories

Meanings: You have so much potential. But are you holding yourself back or letting something else hold you back from tapping into it? Now is the time to free yourself. Reach into your bag of tricks and show the world what it's missing. This angel number is also used to encourage you to collaborate with someone to reach your goals. If you're thinking of starting a business, a podcast, or a YouTube channel with someone else, your angels say it's a great time to try it out. You may also find childhood memories flooding back when you see this angel number. Something may be coming up that you need to face and address. It could also mean that some skill or trait you cultivated as a result of your childhood can help you in your life now.

Affirmation: It's time to team up to build my dream up.

Activation: Full moons are the perfect time to release so you can welcome new energy. When you're trying to tap into your potential, try this to rid yourself of stagnant energy. During a full moon, write down anything that you feel is keeping you from your full potential. In a firesafe container, burn the paper. Ask the full moon to remove these things from your life. Watch as the doors open and your potential is recognized.

Keywords: heightened déjà vu, spiritual evolution,
good news tripled

Meanings: You may experience heightened déjà vu when you see this number. There's something in those moments your angels are trying to bring to your attention. Should you try to do something differently this time? Ask your angels to clarify their message. This angel number also appears when you're going through a spiritual evolution. Maybe you've been at a certain level for a long time. Maybe you haven't grasped certain spiritual concepts before, but now you're about to. Your angels are very proud of your effort. Since 369 contains the number 3, you may be receiving good news three times over. It can also represent expected information, but at a much bigger level than anticipated.

Affirmation: As I grow and change spiritually, I continue to evolve to new levels.

Activation: Whenever you have a moment of déjà vu, pause and reflect on it. What parts feel the most familiar? How much could you recall? How much did you know was about to happen? As you think on the moment, ask your angels to show you more so the overall message is revealed.

Keywords: reunion, everything's falling into place, look to the future

Meanings: A reunion is possible when you see this angel number. This could be with a friend, or a romantic or business partner. This might be a one-time meeting that allows you to end things amicably or leads you to getting back together for the long term. If you're open to a reunion, this is the perfect time for it. Also, when this angel number appears in your life, everything is falling into place. You may feel exactly the opposite at this moment, but trust the process and ride it out. Keep your hopes high. Your angels also send this number when you need to look toward the future. It's important to live in the present, but you must know where you're headed to realize when you get there. Set goals, make a vision board, or try visualization to plan for the future.

Affirmation: Worry is a waste of time because everything's working out just as it should.

Activation: Create a vision board. Cut out images that represent what you want to manifest for your future. Keep the vision board somewhere you can see it each day to keep that future in mind until it becomes reality.

Keywords: learn a new skill, destined for greatness, naturopathy

Meanings: It would be a good time to take a cooking class, head back to college, or even get a new work certification. You will have your angels cheering you on. This angel number is also sent when you're destined for greatness. I've had clients who have gone on to accomplish major goals get a tattoo of this number because they embrace this energy that much. Your angels always want to push you to be your highest self. This angel number is also sent to those who are natural healers. If this resonates with you, look into naturopathy, which is a system of treating disease through natural agents. If you've thought about taking up acupuncture or herbalism, your angels are urging you to do so. Learn more about it. You have a natural gift for the healing arts.

Affirmation: Learning is a lifelong passion.

Activation: Angel number 454 reduces down to the number 4. It represents stability, growth, and understanding. To enhance this number's energy when attaining a new skill, carry four pennies in your right pocket. You'll be surprised how fast you learn whatever it is you're studying.

Keywords: think before you act, amazing nurturer, influential

Meanings: Please think before you act. Take a breath, think about the message you want to convey, and then have a discussion. You may be ready to rush into something immediately, but your angels want you to think about it first. Take a beat, then proceed forward in a calmer state of mind. This angel number is also sent to incredibly nurturing souls. You will see this number when you're thinking of taking a job in the health care or service industry. Your angels say you have the heart of a caregiver, and they support your choice. Also, you are a very influential person when this angel number finds you. You're probably not even aware of how much influence you have on others. People are drawn to you naturally and listen when you speak. Tell them something useful, be it in a blog, a classroom, or a book.

Affirmation: My love for others is reflected in how I care for them.

Activation: When you become overwhelmed or want to react instantly to a situation, take ninety seconds and hit the pause button. Take deep breaths. Walk around to release some of the excess energy. When you speak, you will be in a much better headspace than before.

Keywords: ending bad habits, rainbows, spontaneity

Meanings: It's a good time to release any bad habits or patterns. Maybe it's time to put down the cigarettes or alcohol, especially if you've already felt pulled to do so. Perhaps the people you spend time with aren't good for your mental health. Whatever impairs your ability to be 100 percent needs to be carefully examined at this time. If you've been seeing angel number 545, chances are you'll be seeing rainbows, too. Rainbows are promises of better days ahead. Count the number of rainbows you see once you receive this angel number. It's amazing how different signs from your angels coincide at the same time. The storms in your life will clear when this symbol enters your life. Also, through this number, your angels will urge you to be more spontaneous. Maybe you stick to the tried and true and follow the beaten path. Your angels will push you if it causes you to grow. So, if they want you to act off the cuff a little more, give it a try.

Affirmation: Every moment in life doesn't have to be planned.

Activation: Incorporate rainbow energy into your life. Put a transparent cling rainbow in your window. Paint a room in bright colors. A rainbow is a sign of good things to come after a storm. Use this as inspiration.

565

Meanings: People underestimate you—and they shouldn't. You are capable of much more than they realize. Your angels know this, and they don't want you underestimating yourself. Believe in your abilities. You have your angels at your side no matter what. When you start to see the bigger picture, you will also see this angel number. Or if you need to start looking at a situation as a whole instead of focusing on the details, this angel number will appear. Be careful that you don't get caught up making a bigger deal of smaller issues than needs be. This angel number also finds you when it's time to make some money moves. Almost everything you venture into will score a payday at this time. Make that investment, or play your lucky numbers. You never know what may happen.

Affirmation: I will expand my view to take in the bigger picture.

Activation: If you have felt underestimated by others, or even yourself, find an emblem that can represent a winner. That could be your favorite actor, athlete, or singer. Maybe it's someone in the business or scientific community. You can also find someone who represents an underdog who wins in the end. Having that physical embodiment to look at is inspiring and helps you tap into your own power.

Keywords: highly sensitive, obstacles removed, bluebirds

Meanings: You're a highly sensitive person. You may want to start working with those abilities. Do you feel what others feel? Do you have bigger emotional reactions than most people? Being highly sensitive, although it can feel like a curse at times, is a gift. Start studying and working with your abilities. Also, your angels will send this number when obstacles are being removed from your path. You may have been stuck for a while, but there's a spiritual bulldozer coming in to clear your path now. Also, along with this angel number, you will frequently see bluebirds. These are messengers from loved ones in spirit, frequently from the maternal side of your family. They are coming to say "hello," comfort you, or bring a special "I love you" from heaven.

Affirmation: Obstacles are being removed from my path.

Activation: Add a bluebird figurine to your altar. This can represent one special loved one in spirit or a general connection to the spirit realm. Ask them to send you bluebirds as a "yes" or a "no" to a question. For example, maybe you're considering taking a new job. Ask them to send a bluebird as "yes" or a cardinal for "no." You'll be amazed at how well this works.

Keywords: reinvent yourself, rising confidence, thriving career

Meanings: Time to reinvent yourself. Maybe life has gotten a little stale. Take this as a sign to spice things up. Try a new wardrobe or take up dancing. Whatever is outside your wheelhouse is a perfect place to start. When you have already begun to shake things up in your life, your angels send this as a way to say, "Good for you!" This number will also come up when your confidence begins to rise. Did you recently challenge yourself and come out successful? Did you make yourself proud by pushing beyond your limits? That boost in confidence is a testament to your hard work and determination. Your angels are very proud. Also, when this angel number appears, your career is about to take off. During this phase, you will be very busy, but totally fulfilled by the experience.

Affirmation: I'm loving the new and improved me.

Activation: To sustain a thriving career, invoke the power of the infinity symbol. This symbol makes an excellent tattoo, which certainly keeps the energy with you always. However, for a less permanent option, draw the symbol onto yourself or a piece of paper and carry it with you. Also, jewelry with an infinity symbol charm or clothing that contains the symbol will work to enhance this energy.

Keywords: switch it up, selflessness, new path opening

Meanings: If you've been questioning whether you should switch up your routine, the answer is yes. Change your diet, sense of style, home, or job. Bring in some fresh energy! You are also a selfless person when your angels send this number. You have given yourself over to helping people, and it hasn't gone unnoticed by your angels. Make sure to show yourself the same care and love you do for others, however. This angel number will also show up when there's a new path opening. You can still reach your goals, but your angels are asking you to see another route to success. They will also work on opening another way for you as well. Many roads can lead to the same destination.

Affirmation: Bring on the fresh energy!

Activation: To make sure that you don't lose your self-identity when helping others, practice this mantra. A mantra is a repetitious phrase imbued with spiritual powers. In this case, repeat the following before heading into a situation to care for others or any time you feel as though you may lose yourself: "My sense of self remains with me. I love others, but first comes me." This is not a proclamation of pride, but an anchoring statement to center you.

Keywords: redoubling effort, twice blessed, peaceful resolution

Meanings: It's time to redouble your efforts. Your angels send this when you're close to reaching a goal, but need to make a final push to get there. Your efforts are also being redoubled by the fact that you're receiving help from your angels. With angelic backup, you're sure to accomplish whatever task stands before you. Also, this angel number resonates with being twice blessed. I had a client who received this angel number when she found out she was expecting twins. This angel number also appears when winnings are doubled or what was expected is much more than anticipated. When there is a peaceful resolution possible for a problem you're having with someone, you will see this angel number. It may have seemed impossible, but when your angels step in, things inevitably take a turn for the positive.

Affirmation: This situation will be resolved calmly and peacefully.

Activation: Wherever you work, whether at home or in an office among coworkers, add this to the room to help redouble your efforts. Doubling the intensity requires more strength. To represent that added strength, buy a couple of five-pound dumbbells. Place one at either side of the door to your office. Let them remain there until you've finished the situation that required the extra elbow grease.

Keywords: teach others, rapid revolution, auspicious timing

Meanings: You need to step up and teach people what you know. This may mean that you're currently in school to become a teacher or maybe you have special skills that others would benefit from. Don't sell yourself short. You have a gift for taking a complicated subject and simplifying it for others to grasp. You will also see rapid revolution in your life when this angel number appears. It could start with a dream that makes you rethink everything you've ever known. It could be something you overhear that leads you to make radical changes to your way of life. Your angels support you in this endeavor. Receiving this angel number also signals a great time to get things done. The timing is auspicious, which means it is likely to be successful. So, when this number pops up, consider it the time to get married, start a business, or take classes.

Affirmation: I'm happy to teach my skills to others.

Activation: As this number reduces to the number 22, you can channel its auspicious energy by starting a project twenty-two minutes after the hour. For example, send your resume at 8:22 a.m., or wake up each day at 6:22 a.m. to incorporate that energy throughout your entire day. Watch how much more smoothly those tasks go when you do. Use this technique to add a little extra luck to almost any activity.

Keywords: sudden shift, challenging moment, soul support

Meanings: A sudden shift is occurring in your life. This could be a personal breakthrough you experience or an outside influence that will change your situation. Your angels don't want you to worry. Most times, knowing the information beforehand helps eliminate fear surrounding it. This angel number may also come to you when there is a challenging moment ahead. Certain events cannot be avoided, but they're here to teach and inform you while on earth. Although your angels know this is a challenging moment for you, they see the bigger picture, and are here to help get you through it. You are also receiving soul support when this angel number is sent. You never walk this journey alone, although we tend to believe that fallacy while on earth. We forget the soul contract we made before coming to this planet, but your angels don't. They will walk with you and support you no matter what you face.

Affirmation: Although this may be difficult to deal with, I know I'm never alone on my journey.

Activation: Whenever you're facing a challenging time in life, use a little tulsi, or holy basil, to get you through it. In the world of natural medicine, tulsi has been found to have health-improving properties, and on the spiritual side, you can use it to help calm you and improve your meditations while dealing with hard times.

Keywords: working with Saraswati, go with the flow, liberation

Meanings: Saraswati is a Hindu goddess who represents creativity, music, and education. When you receive this angel number, her presence may be entering your life in order for you to work with her energy. She is said to have a calming presence and can help you when life feels otherwise chaotic. Your angels will also send this number when you need to go with the flow. Maybe things have been difficult, and you're in an uphill battle. Instead of continuing to fight against the tide, your angels' advice is to go with it instead. The resolution will come that much sooner. This angel number also lets you know when you're about to experience liberation in your life. If you've struggled with substance abuse or other bad habits, this message should buoy your spirits. Your angels are with you. They will help liberate you from either a bad situation, person, or habit in your life.

Affirmation: Better to flow with the current than swim against the tide.

Activation: Purchase a statue of Saraswati and place her on your altar. Offer her sweets and fruits, such as mango or dessert. Also, place yellow on your altar as it's her favorite color.

989

Meanings: You're being commended on your compassionate heart. You most likely have recently shown the strength of your heart, and your angels are giving you a standing ovation. Your kindness makes the world a brighter place. There also may be some secrets revealed that others have kept from you when you see this angel number. You will now see a situation for what it is and not how it's been portrayed. This angel number also represents the ascended master Krishna, the Hindu god of protection, tenderness, and love. When this deity enters your energetic space, you will feel protected and loved.

Affirmation: My empathy for others fulfills my purpose and fills my soul.

Activation: As Krishna was the eighth incarnation of Vishnu, Hindu god of preservation, this deity resonates with the energy of eight that angel number 989 reduces to (9 + 8 + 9 = 26; 2 + 6 = 8). Add a Krishna statue to your altar or sacred space. He can appear in several forms, from a baby to a young lover. Choose which you identify with most strongly and which energies you want to work with. Having a physical focus to work with can help you channel this energy more clearly.

1212

Meanings: Don't worry another minute about any injustice you've suffered. All is seen, and all will be dealt with at the right time. Give that worry over to a higher power to handle. Justice will be served in your life. Your angels will also send this number when you have the ability to channel Moses energy. According to Judaism, Moses was chosen as God's lawgiver. You may be called to be a leader at this time. Step into the role. You'll have extra help while you do. Also, it's likely you've recently gone through or will go through a mindset shift. Perhaps you're ready to move past some old trauma. Maybe your ideas about a situation have changed suddenly. Your angels are confirming this was important for you to do.

Affirmation: I trust that justice will be served.

Activation: When you have an issue requiring justice to be served, grab a tarot deck. In the major arcana, the eleventh card is the justice card. This card represents karma doing her thing, taking care of those who have hurt others. You won't have to do a thing other than watch it all happen, popcorn at the ready. Carry it in your wallet or purse. Put it in your pocket or on your altar. This will help the issue be resolved that much sooner.

1357

Keywords: cosmic experiences, Fatimah encounter, different path

Meanings: Cosmic experiences, such as interactions with angels, spirits, and even extraterrestrials, are possible at this time. These experiences can go hand in hand with visions and spiritual downloads. A loss of time during these interactions is also possible. Your angels will guide you and keep you grounded. You will also see this number when it's possible to have a Fatimah encounter. Fatimah was the only daughter of the prophet Muhammad and his first wife, Khadija. She is respected among Muslims as she supported her father after her mother's death. If your energy matches hers, she will enter your life to help you not only care for others, but also for yourself. This number also appears when you're about to head down a different path, most likely one you didn't plan to take. That doesn't mean you won't get where you want to go. You may just have to take the scenic route, however, to get there.

Affirmation: I'm open to out-of-this world experiences.

Activation: Whether having visions or being visited in dreams by significant religious figures, this type of activity can make you feel a little detached from the real world. The key to get through this and receive all you can from the experience is to center yourself. During this time, meditate, go outside and ground, and try this. Go outside on a particularly sunny day. Stand facing the sun with arms extended, palms up. Let the sun's rays penetrate the chakras in your palms and absorb their life-giving energy. This will energize and stabilize you.

Keywords: self-reflection, perseverance, Archangel Michael

Meanings: You're either doing some self-reflection or you need to. Your angels want to encourage you to continue to travel in that light as it will help you resolve issues. Going within is always a positive. Your perseverance is also being encouraged when this angel number shows up. Your angels encourage you to keep going—life hasn't been easy, but they want to reassure you that they're always there for you. This special angel number also resonates with the energy of Archangel Michael. You may need a warrior spirit in your life. With his presence, you're getting a boost from his energy to help you through a difficult time.

Affirmation: Persevering tells the Universe I'm still here, and I won't give up.

Activation: Archangel Michael is a powerful protector. You can place his statue in your home, office, or even your car. Ask him to help you with particularly difficult situations. He will do the fighting for you. Also, focusing on his statue helps strengthen your resolve and tenacity in tough times.

2323

Keywords: Archangel Raphael, true connection, brave first step

Meanings: Archangel Raphael is coming into your life. This archangel represents healing and a safe passage on journeys. You most likely have some healing to do when Archangel Raphael shows up. He will help you through it. When you're about to experience true connection, 2323 will appear. This connection can be with another person, yourself, or even a higher power. Something about the relationships you're in will connect in a way not experienced before. Also, your angels want to remind you that you're never alone, especially when you're about to take a step into new territory. This can indicate that you're going to take a step toward a healthier lifestyle, make yourself a priority, or do something that challenges you. Your angels hold your hand as you take that first step.

Affirmation: Doing something while afraid is the definition of bravery.

Activation: Before making a big change or taking the first step toward a new situation, carry two nickels to invoke this angel number's correlation with bravery. As this angel number breaks down into 55, carrying double nickels channels that energy.

Keywords: deeper understanding, Archangel Uriel, discernment

Meanings: You're receiving a deeper understanding of a subject. This can come in the form of a revelation that helps you see what transpired more clearly. It can also mean, through study and practice, you're reaching a deeper understanding of your spiritual beliefs. You're going through an enlightening experience that will enrich your life. This angel number also appears when Archangel Uriel's energy is available to work with. He's an angel of wisdom and represents thunder and lightning. There are insights possible and learning that can take place when you channel his energy. Your angels will also make you aware that you have the gift of discernment with this angel number. Discernment is the ability to judge people and situations well, almost as if you have an insider's view. Your angels encourage you to develop and hone this skill.

Affirmation: My understanding of this situation has deepened greatly.

Activation: If you'd like to elevate your discernment, find a piece of rainbow fluorite. This crystal stabilizes and brings clarity of mind. You can place the crystal on your altar, hold it while meditating, and/or carry it on you when you need a little more insight into a situation.

Keywords: breaking away, unity, Archangel Gabriel

Meanings: You truly are your own person when you receive this angel number. You have or are in the process of breaking away from situations that no longer serve you, jobs that are holding you back, or generational issues that stop with you. This is a time to celebrate your independence. Your angels have your back but marvel at how you stand independently. This angel number is also sent when there's a sense of unity moving into your life. You may feel more in tune with a romantic or business partner. A relationship with a child or parent could also start to feel more united than ever before. Things are clicking, and everyone is on the same page. The Archangel Gabriel is being sent your way when you receive this angel number. He is known as the messenger angel. He comes with news straight from God. When this angel number appears, it brings an energy you need more of into your life.

Affirmation: I break from tradition to do what feels best for me.

Activation: To symbolize and enhance your breaking-away moment, find a stick, one thin enough to break and long enough to break several times. Because this angel number breaks down to 10, let's incorporate that into the exercise. Speak aloud that which you are breaking away from and snap the limb. Do that nine more times, and on the last break, toss the remaining piece over your left shoulder. Feel how free you feel. Over the coming weeks, feel the freedom in your body and see whether the break is clean and beautiful.

Keywords: greater responsibility, smooth sailing, make a plan

Meanings: You will be taking on greater responsibility. This could be more responsibility at work with a possible promotion. There could be more responsibility with an addition to your family, be it human or fur baby variety. Your angels want you to know that you're ready for the challenge. This angel number also comes when you're about to enter a peaceful period. No matter your current situation, things are soon to become much easier. When this angel number finds you, you need to make a plan. Maybe you're flying by the seat of your pants. Your angels say you need a little more structure. Create a plan to ensure you achieve your goals.

Affirmation: I'm up to the task of taking on greater responsibility in my life.

Activation: If planning isn't your thing, try this method. Using the 3434 angel number as a guide, write down three things you need to do. Give yourself four ways to get each done. Then, to reward yourself and encourage you to do this again in the future, write down three treats for getting those things done and four different forms those treats can take.

3579

Meanings: You may have an issue with anger that needs to be addressed. Perhaps there are some things you've suppressed, and they're boiling to the surface now. If this resonates with you, anger management therapy is always an option. Remember, it's perfectly natural to become angry, but to stay in that anger is not healthy. Your angels will also send this number if you've been holding in your feelings too long. You need to release that emotional baggage. If you can't address the person directly, try therapeutic measures to unburden yourself. This angel number is also used to bring your artistic ability into the spotlight. You have real talent. Maybe you deny it. Maybe you don't feel supported, but when you receive this angel number, it's time to share your art with the world.

Affirmation: Anger is a valid emotion, but I won't let it control me.

Activation: To channel your inner artist and let those talents shine, find a statue of Athena. Athena was the Greek goddess and patroness of all art forms. So, no matter which art form you practice, she will be a guiding light for you. Place her near wherever you create your art.

Keywords: rejuvenation, bountiful, on the right track

Meanings: You've reached a stage of rejuvenation. Higher levels of awareness and spirituality have given you a good foundation. Through that process, your soul has been rejuvenated and given you a boost. Enjoy this blissful feeling. You earned it. You're also about to enter a bountiful period when you see this angel number. If you own a business, revenues will be through the roof. If you're in a relationship, love is off the charts. Bounty and beauty will flood your life. You'll also receive this angel number when you've been worried about making the right choices and being on the right path. You're definitely on the right track. Keep moving forward on this path, and let the worries go.

Affirmation: I'm entering a phase of soul rejuvenation.

Activation: Buy yourself a money tree to keep that bounty flowing, especially for finances. This beautiful houseplant known formally as *Pachira aquatica*, or water chestnut, is said to bring more money into your life. Some people will clip bills to the leaves, but the safest technique is to place a few paper money bills and some coins at the base of the flower pot. The more it grows, the more your bounty grows.

Keywords: reconsider, culmination, party time

Meanings: Your angels are asking you to reconsider something. It could be a recent decision you've made. Perhaps someone is asking for another chance with you. Think about reconsidering. If you still feel firm about your decision, stay with it. But if you feel as though you want to change your mind, you're being supported to do that. This angel number also represents reaching a culmination in your life. You'll see this when you're nearing the end of a project, like an upcoming graduation, wedding, or other significant event. Your angels are cheering you on. Speaking of celebrating, this number is also sent when you need to party. Let your hair down and dance the night away. Life is serious. Remember to have some fun.

Affirmation: I'm flexible enough to change my mind when new information presents itself.

Activation: This may not be the most sacred ritual I've included in this book, but it's one of the most fun. No matter what day of the week it is or what you have going on, buy yourself a birthday cake. Life is always better with cake. You don't need a major reason to buy it. It doesn't even have to be your birthday. Nobody's going to know. Go get that cake and enjoy yourself to the fullest.

Keywords: alone not lonely, feeling seen, allowing

Meanings: There are moments in life that require time alone, but being alone doesn't necessarily equate to being lonely. Others in your life may not understand your choices, but your angels do, and they are with you on this journey. Your angels will also use this number when you're about to receive the emotional fulfillment of being seen. Each of us wants to feel as though at least one other person on this planet sees us for the true soul we are. When this number appears, you will enjoy that experience. Your angels also want to commend you on simply allowing life to come at you. You're learning how to be in flow, and they want to recognize you for that.

Affirmation: Time alone centers and invigorates me.

Activation: When you want to be in flow with life, try a sensory deprivation tank. This is a lightless, soundless tank filled with just enough water and Epsom salts to create the sensation of floating. Putting yourself in this state enhances your ability to simply allow and not fight against life's flow.

Keywords: blissful, Higher Self alignment, releasing expectations

Meanings: You're entering a state of bliss. It's a beautiful period where life is sweet, and things work out as you'd hoped. This is one of those rare moments in life, so your angels want you to enjoy every minute of it. You will also see this number when you've moved into alignment with your Higher Self and you're walking your true path. The moves you're making are in tune with what you planned before you ever came to earth. This number also appears when you're releasing expectations, which is a good thing. Expecting or assuming something will work out in a certain way limits all other ways of reaching your goals. So when you set an intention, work toward a goal but release the need to control the outcome. You may receive this shout-out from your angels.

Affirmation: I release the need to control the outcome.

Activation: Since the angel number 5656 is another form of 1111, try this check-in to keep in flow with your Higher Self. Whenever you see 11:11, in the morning or at night, do this simple realignment. Say aloud, "If I'm not in alignment with my Higher Self, help correct my course." If there are some things you should tweak to get back into alignment, you'll notice your habits subtly change, or your thoughts slightly shift. Once you let the Universe know you want to be in flow, your angels will get you back on track.

Keywords: adding structure, divine love, faith tested

Meanings: You need to add some structure to your routine when you see this angel number. Maybe you've become a little blasé and are letting some things slide that shouldn't. Your angels will nudge you gently to firm up those routines. You're also being sent divine love when you receive this angel number. You might feel this in meditations or quiet walks in nature. Your angels love and care for you. Sometimes, they simply send a little extra your way to remind you. This angel number will also appear when your faith is being tested. It's not that you've been sent a challenge or test to overcome but rather a learning experience to work your way through. You're not alone in the fight.

Affirmation: Structure offers me a starting framework.

Activation: Call on Joan of Arc energy to keep your faith high. Hang her picture or find a statue to place on your altar. It can be argued that Joan of Arc's faith was second to none. When you call on this energy, your faith will receive a helping hand.

Keywords: physical release, negative self-talk,
expanding knowledge

Meanings: The body keeps a running tabulation of everything you go through. Emotions and energies can get trapped within the body. So, those energies need to be released before becoming a bigger problem. Try hip stretch releases, yoga, or other modalities that get the physical body to open up and release those old traumas. This will aid healing. Your angels will also send this number when you've been too hard on yourself. Are you listening to that negative voice in your head? Have you been tearing yourself down? Your angels can't tolerate it when you're mean to yourself, so cut it out and give yourself more love. You will also see this angel number when your knowledge on a subject is expanding. This can appear when you've signed up for a seminar or class or are earning a college degree. This refers to self-teaching as well. Learn all that you can!

Affirmation: Even on my hard days, I choose to be loving to myself.

Activation: Try out deep stretches or yoga to tap into a physical release. You can also accomplish this through several martial arts including jujitsu or Tai Chi. Don't worry if physical movements cause emotional reactions. That's exactly what's supposed to happen and is how the body releases old traumas.

7676

Keywords: appreciated, prosperity, inner pride

Meanings: Get ready for your moment in the sun when you receive this angel number. You're about to receive the appreciation you so richly deserve. Your angels always appreciate you, but it is nice to feel appreciated by those in your life, too. This is also an excellent angel number for prosperity. Investments you've made will pay off or sudden windfalls will find you when you see this angel number. Make sure to set some aside. You can build upon this money. The number 7676 will also find you when your inner pride is growing. This is a big personal achievement when your angels acknowledge it. You may have struggled with self-esteem issues in the past and, so, to reach a new level of inner confidence is something to be excited about. Don't worry about patting yourself on the back. You've earned it.

Affirmation: I can be proud of myself without being full of myself.

Activation: Flowing water has always been a sign of abundance. To call it into your life, try this. If you can find a natural source of flowing water, such as a brook or stream, that's great. However, you can also achieve this at your kitchen sink. Put your hands beneath the water as it flows from the faucet, or into the stream, and say, "As water flows with peace and ease so, too, does prosperity flow to me." Repeat it at least four times and as often as you'd like.

7878

Keywords: inner strength, composure, break in the action

Meanings: Your angels are acknowledging the inner strength you possess. They love that you have come through so much and, yet, still have a caring heart. That inner strength has served you well. You've withstood storms that would have broken others' spirits. You're being commended for that. If you're leaning on that inner strength right now, your angels see that. You're not alone. You will also receive this message from your angels to encourage you to keep your composure. Don't let someone bring you down to their level. Stay true to yourself. The Universe will handle that annoying person. Your angels also send this number when there's going to be a break in the action. You've most likely been going, going, going. Well, now it's time to take a break. Revel in the peace.

Affirmation: I won't let someone else's actions determine how I respond.

Activation: There's a perfect card in the tarot that addresses inner strength. It's the strength card. Clever, right? It traditionally depicts a woman holding a lion's mouth, subduing the king of the jungle. She doesn't do it with brute force, but through her ability to finesse the situation. Carry this card on you or place it on your altar if you'd like to enhance your inner strength.

8787

Meanings: You're about to break some real records. You're most likely a trailblazer, and your angels want to acknowledge that. You're forging a path for those who will follow you. That's a big responsibility, but you're more than capable. You will also see your hard work pay off when you receive this angel number. You've been pushing for a long time. It's not been in vain. Also, Triple Goddess energy is coming when you see this number. She represents the maiden, mother, and crone. This persona is represented in the phases of the moon. She embodies the life cycle of a woman. This tends to show up when you're going through a transitional period. You can use the Triple Goddess's energy to help you manage your life.

Affirmation: I blaze a path so others can travel this trail as well.

Activation: The Triple Goddess imagery can be found in many forms, from statues to paintings. If you want to incorporate this energy into your magical work or your life in general, place those likenesses on your altar or bedside table. You can also do this with the phases of the moon and allow that symbology to represent the same thing. The Triple Goddess is helpful during a woman's transition periods of menses, perimenopause, and menopause.

8989

Keywords: spiritual wake-up call, self-assured, go deeper

Meanings: You're receiving a spiritual wake-up call. You may have turned away from your spiritual practice, but your angels are asking you to take another look. You're missing something in your life that spiritual fulfillment can help with. When you see this number, you're also feeling more confident. You carry yourself a little taller, as you should. Your angels love to see your growth. When your angels want to push you deeper into your spirituality or learning a certain subject, you'll see 8989. This shows up when you've started something but are running out of gas and need some motivation to keep going. Let this serve as your second wind and dig deeper.

Affirmation: I step into my confidence and wear it proudly.

Activation: Use labradorite to help you reconnect with your spirituality as well as deepen your understanding of certain subjects. This beautiful crystal brings mental clarity as well as mystical experiences. Wear it as jewelry or place a piece somewhere on your person.

9898

Keywords: magical moment, spiritual push, making new friends

Meanings: You're about to experience a magical moment when your angels send this number. This could be contact with a spirit, extraterrestrial, or even a cryptid, like Bigfoot or a mermaid. This can also imply a certain moment that feels so special you'll never forget it. Your angels will also send this number to give you a spiritual push. They're always there, and sometimes we take that for granted. They want you to know you have their blessing on your path. Now, get to it. This is also a great sign for making new friends. You might be taking a class or making a connection online that brings new people into your life, usually when you least expect it. These are quality people being sent by your angels. Open up and welcome new friends into your life.

Affirmation: I'm open to magic in my life in whatever form it takes.

Activation: If you need a friend, and who doesn't nowadays, carry the angel number 9898 on you to increase social connections and friendliness with others. If you work from home and don't get out much to socialize, write 9898 on a sticky note and place it on your laptop. Friends come in all forms these days, and we can all use extra help finding them.

PERSONAL TO YOU

These numbers are special because of their meaning to you. What is your birth date? What day did you get married? What's your Social Security or driver's license number? These numbers follow us for life, but are different and unique to each of us. For that reason, your angels will use them to send messages.

When you see your birth date repeatedly, it's time to pause and reflect on where you're headed. Your angels are asking you to think about your life's path. Do you feel as though you're headed in the right direction? Are there changes you'd like to make? Seeing your birth date gives you a moment to reassess where you are and where you want to be.

As for other special dates and numbers unique to you, take note of what's going on in your life when you see these numbers frequently. This is an excellent way to communicate with your angels. Perhaps the date you graduated high school or college always pops up when something's ending, like a job or relationship. Your angels aren't sending it to make you feel badly that something's over. They do it to remind you that, like graduation, you've finished a chapter, and there's something new and exciting coming your way.

Keep a journal or a notes file in your phone open to jot down any recurring personal angel numbers you receive. These angel numbers are the most special and unique to you, and they can set a strong foundation for you to learn how to better communicate with your angels.

CHAPTER 5

INCORPORATING ANGEL NUMBERS INTO DAILY LIFE

FOR THE MOST part, angel numbers are seen as a receptive or passive experience. You're going about your business, then, out of nowhere, you receive a message from your angels. But did you know you can make angel numbers a much more active experience? Let me show you a few ways to use angel numbers to speak with your angels, schedule important events, and even manifest your greatest desires!

First up, angel numbers aren't just a vehicle for your angels to communicate to *you*. They can be used for you to communicate to *them* as well. You can choose a specific angel number and use it as a confirmation. For example, let's say you have a big decision to make. Now, again, your angels can never interfere with your free will, but they can advise if something is more aligned with your higher purpose. You're toying with a job change. You haven't been happy in a long time, and secretly you've always longed to be an artist. But we live in a world in which bills must be paid and obligations met. So, you're hesitant to make the change. You decide that 333 is going to be your confirmation to make the crucial change. Be specific when you set this up so you won't discount seeing the number as a simple coincidence. Advise your angels that if you're supposed to quit your current job and pursue your dream of art, you will see the number 333 at least three times within the next 24 hours. That gives a very specific parameter, and even the most skeptical person would have to agree is proof that the message has been sent from your angels. This is one scenario. Talk to your angels as often as you need, and you'll find that angel numbers are an excellent way to set up two-way communication between you and them.

Another excellent use of angel numbers is that of divine timing. Let's say you're due to get married next spring. Of course, you want that day to be as special as possible. Maybe you highly resonate with the number 4 or consider 44 to be a personal lucky number. Then, perhaps you'd like to get married on April 4 or the fourth of any spring month. You can also add up the numbers of the date and, regardless of whether the actual day is a 4, if the number adds up in total to a 4 or 44, then it would be a great day to get married. You can use this technique to schedule other important events such as elective surgeries (as long as it's not an emergency and your doctor agrees), salon appointments, parties, or, really, any date you consider important that you'd like an extra dose of good vibes for.

Last, but certainly not least, angel numbers are excellent mediums for manifesting. Manifestation is the act of bringing something into your life through focused intention and inspired action. Once you've decided what you want to bring into your life, pick an angel number that represents it. The number 777 would be great for luck. For quicker manifestation, 1111 would be excellent. For getting prayers answered, use 222. Place angel numbers on your vision board or an altar you've created for your manifestations. Use them as a focal point during meditations or visualizations. Having a specific reference helps manifest your desires more quickly. Angel numbers vibrate at a certain frequency that, when tapped in to, can bring about manifestations much more quickly and intensely.

CONCLUSION

Who knew angel numbers were so versatile? They not only convey messages of hope, comfort, and pride, but also assist in manifesting, confirming choices, and even picking the right dates for life's most important moments. My hope is that you find this book to be a great resource to reference repeatedly when your guardian spirits send these magical numbers your way. Whenever you're in doubt, need a pat on the back, or need a sign for which way to go, you now have the tools to communicate with your angels. It is my wish that this is the start of a beautiful relationship between you and your angels as you'll have a greater understanding of the messages you're receiving.

And since you've learned how special these numbers can be in your life, let me give you one more—145. These are my initials in number form. Anytime you see this number, know it's my way of saying "thank you" for letting me play a small part in your spiritual journey.

ACKNOWLEDGMENTS

Thank you to my dear editor, John Foster, who helped guide this series into all it could be. I am forever in your debt. I also want to acknowledge and thank the entire team at Weldon Owen. My experience with you has never been anything but top-notch. Thank you, Kayla Belser, for all of your hard work and encouragement. Of course, I want to thank my husband and children for their love and support. They are my biggest cheerleaders and greatest inspirations. I must also give a huge thank you to my online community at Namaste Magical. My work wouldn't be possible without you. Last, but certainly not least, I have to express my gratitude to Spirit, who I know conspired from beyond the veil to bring all of this to fruition. Thank you from the bottom of my heart. I hope this work makes you proud.

ABOUT THE AUTHOR

 April Wall is an international psychic medium with twenty years of experience helping clients sort through life's ups and downs. A proud Romany, she carries on the traditions started by the strong women in her family, especially her great-grandmother, great-aunt, and granny, or as she refers to them, April's Angels. She lives with her husband, two kids, two doggies, and one spoiled kitty. Find her online at *NamasteMagical.com* to book a reading, and keep up to date through her social media accounts by following her on Instagram and TikTok @namastemagical.

ALSO BY APRIL WALL
IN THE DAILY DIVINATION SERIES:

Reading Tea Leaves   *Reading Tarot*
ISBN: 979-8-88674-007-3   ISBN: 979-8-88674-009-7

weldon**owen**

an imprint of Insight Editions
P.O. Box 3088
San Rafael, CA 94912
www.weldonowen.com

CEO Raoul Goff
VP Publisher Roger Shaw
Editorial Director Katie Killebrew
Senior Editor John Foster
Editorial Assistant Kayla Belser
VP Creative Chrissy Kwasnik
Art Director Allister Fein
VP Manufacturing Alix Nicholaeff
Sr Production Manager Joshua Smith
Sr Production Manager, Subsidiary Rights Lina s Palma-Temena

Weldon Owen would also like to thank Mary Cassells for copyediting
and Bob Cooper for proofreading.

ISBN: 979-8-88674-103-2

Manufactured in China by Insight Editions
10 9 8 7 6 5 4 3 2 1